The Handbook
for Focus Group
Research

The Handbook for Focus Group Research

Revised and Expanded Edition

Thomas L. Greenbaum

Lexington Books
An Imprint of Macmillan, Inc.
NEW YORK
Maxwell Macmillan Canada
TORONTO
Maxwell Macmillan International
NEW YORK OXFORD SiNGAPORE SYDNEY

Library of Congress Cataloging-in-Publication Data

Greenbaum, Thomas L.
    The handbook for focus group research / Thomas L. Greenbaum.
Rev. and expanded ed.
     p. cm.
    Rev. ed. of: The practical handbook and guide to focus group
research. ©1988.
    Includes index.
    ISBN 0–669–27799–1
    1. Marketing research. 2. Focused group interviewing.
  I. Greenbaum, Thomas L. Practical handbook and guide to focus
group research. II. Title.
    HF5415.2.G695 1993
    658.8′ 3—dc20   92–38160
                                                CIP

Lexington Books
An Imprint of Macmillan, Inc.
866 Third Avenue, New York, N.Y. 10022

Maxwell Macmillan Canada, Inc.
1200 Eglinton Avenue East
Suite 200
Don Mills, Ontario M3C 3N1

Macmillan, Inc. is part of the Maxwell Communication
Group of Companies.

Printed in the United States of America

printing number
1 2 3 4 5 6 7 8 9 10

To my mother, Adele Leblang Greenbaum:
She always ran the show—and the reviews were great!
Her courage has been an inspiration.

Contents

Foreword

Perhaps no technique for gaining useful information in the world of business generally, and in the arena of marketing specifically, has been used more often—sometimes successfully, sometimes unsuccessfully—than focus groups. And perhaps no technique has been as controversial and as misunderstood as focus groups. As a young account executive in the advertising business in the 1960s, I remember vividly, and with a chuckle, two clients at the same company who were working on the same brand. One client relied extensively on focus groups to help with decision making, while the other dismissed such groups as "unreliable" and "unprojectable." Had the nay-sayer had the benefit of the thinking, processes, and experiences contained in Tom Greenbaum's first book, *The Practical Handbook and Guide to Focus Group Research*, he would have been instantly converted into a strong believer in focus groups as an indispensable and enormously beneficial step in gathering usable and pertinent information on which to base strategic and executional decisions. As it turned out, the supporter of focus groups did prevail, and he and I continued to use groups productively for our brand.

Conducting focus groups that result in useful information, insights, and perspectives requires both science and art. And in my experience, only a handful of practitioners understand the science and can intuitively grasp the art of conducting them. Tom Greenbaum clearly heads up the list of these few. In many ways, this is a "how-to" book that provides the reader with a conceptual framework for understanding the processes that should be followed to produce successful results. The depth of knowledge of focus groups reflected in this book is not only truly astounding but is clearly articulated. I cannot imagine a reader not finding herein new thoughts about focus groups or, more important, ideas of specific applications for the reader's business. For the practitioner, this book provides new ways to elicit even better results for clients from focus groups.

In the 1990s, in my own business of marketing and marketing communications, focus group research is absolutely indispensable for staying close to consumers and their ever-shifting attitudes, emotions, thoughts, and buying impulses. Tom Greenbaum conducts many focus groups for our company, based on the principles and techniques outlined originally in *The Practical Handbook and Guide to Focus Group Research* and expanded on significantly in the new information provided about moderating focus groups which are presented in this book. Without these groups, we would not be able to create the kind of business-building communications programs that our clients demand.

The world of business is moving more rapidly today than ever before. Hence, we all need information to come faster and to be more reliable. Tom Greenbaums newest book on focus groups is an excellent supplement to *The Practical Handbook and Guide to Focus Group Research* as it presents a compelling argument which suggests that the increased use of focus groups, if organized and conducted properly, can lead to better decisions more quickly made for businesses.

Roy Bostock
Chairman and CEO
D'Arcy Masius Benton & Bowles, Inc.

Introduction

"Let's do some groups!" Six years ago, when I began writing *The Practical Handbook and Guide to Focus Group Research,* this was a very common cry among product and marketing managers and market researchers. My objective at that time was to produce the definitive book on focus group research, since I had found that in the vast reams of market research literature, there was no single text that covered all the aspects of the focus group technique that are needed to use focus groups most effectively.

The intent of my first book was to provide users of qualitative market research with some basic guidelines that would help them determine when focus groups are and are not appropriate to meet their research objectives and to provide a reference book for moderators who want to learn all the important details involved in implementing focus groups. I felt that the focus group technique was being misused by many organizations, and my hope was that the information contained in my first book would help researchers determine when to use them and when other research methods would be more appropriate in the light of their research objectives.

I am pleased to report that the first book has been very successful, both in terms of the absolute sales it has generated to date (it is now in its seventh printing, and late in 1990 it was released in a paperback edition) and in terms of the reception it has received throughout the marketing and market research community. At the present time, most major corporations have *The Practical Handbook and Guide to Focus Group Research* in their libraries; many universities use the book in their marketing and market research curricula; and a large number of marketing and market research personnel all over the English-speaking world have read the book. Further, the reviews in such prestigious industry publications such as *The Journal of Marketing Research, Quirk's,* and *American Banker* have been extremely favorable and helped the book gain exposure in its early days.

In light of this success, many people have asked me why I would want to write a second book on focus groups, and even more important, why people would purchase another book on this very specialized research topic. Clearly, at the time I wrote the first book, I had no intention of following it up with a new and expanded version at a later date. Who would have thought that a topic like focus groups would warrant a follow-up? Who would have thought that so much would happen in only five years that a new and completely different book on the topic would be justified?

The answers to these questions lie basically in the evolution of the focus group research technique since 1986, when I first began writing the book. In 1986, focus groups were an extremely popular research technique and were probably the most commonly used type of market research used in America. But as happens with so many aspects of marketing and market research, the extreme popularity and frequent use of the technique in the late 1980s caused clients to demand increasingly more from focus groups. As a result, many very important changes have been made in focus group research in the last several years that have motivated me to write this second book.

Among the most important of these are first, that a *new type of moderator* has emerged in the 1990s, different from the type evident in the 1980s. The new moderator is much more likely to be a full-time qualitative researcher who devotes his or her career to focus groups, one-on-ones, dyads (perhaps), and maybe some meeting facilitation work as an adjunct to research. Further, this person is more likely to have a marketing background than to come into the qualitative research industry via traditional market research channels.

A second important change is that *many new techniques of moderation* have been developed over the past several years, all aimed at helping moderators elicit more valuable information from participants. These need to be exposed to the practitioners in the industry so everyone can benefit from this new learning.

Third, there has been *a greater recognition of the importance of the moderator* as the leader of the focus group process. Client organizations spend considerably more time and effort now in finding the best moderator for their projects than they did in the mid-1980s. No longer do researchers in a corporate environment retain just anyone who claims to know how to moderate. Most clients now have enough experience with focus groups to be able to discriminate between qualified and unqualified moderators and to know which moderators can provide "value added" by virtue of their own techniques, their past experience, or their particular skills in interviewing or interpreting the results.

Fourth, *a large number of new applications of focus groups* have emerged that were not common in the early 1980s. These include extensive work with the medical profession, as drug companies develop new products and the marketing programs to sell them. It also includes work with industrial clients, where focus groups are conducted to assist in business-to-business marketing of all types of products and services. The nonprofit sector has also begun to use focus groups more than before. Finally, the focus group technique has become common in the legal profession as a vehicle to help litigators improve the overall quality of the cases they are preparing for trial. This expansion of focus groups has brought new challenges and opportunities to the industry, as the techniques that were traditionally employed with "normal" consumers had to be modified somewhat to be appropriate for many of the new participant segments.

Fifth, *the demands that clients and moderators make on research facilities have changed.* Researchers have come to understand the need for more professional recruiting, better physical plants, and more of a partnership between the moderator, the client, and the focus group facility. At the present time, the weakest link in the focus group chain is probably the facility. The next few years will see more pressure put on facilities to offer the same level of professionalism that is presently available from many of the better moderators in the United States.

Finally, some *important technological changes* over the past five years have also affected the focus group industry and will continue to impact on it. These technological changes include remote, two-way broadcasts from facilities to client offices; satellite technology applied to focus groups on both a national and an international level; database matching of recruits, to minimize the proliferation of "professional" respondents; and the application of telephone conferencing to focus groups.

This book is an attempt to bridge the gap between the mid-1980s literature on focus groups and the state of the industry in 1992. It contains mostly new material that was not covered in my initial effort, although there is necessarily some repetition of background material. Still, most of what this book covers is new and completely additive to the information contained in *The Practical Handbook and Guide to Focus Group Research*. If you have not read that book, I strongly urge you to obtain a copy, as it is a very important introduction to the topic of focus groups and would certainly enhance your understanding of the material in this book.

As you look through the index of this book, you will recognize the more advanced nature of the material covered here, compared with the first book. For example, in this book, I provide information on the following important topics:

1. How to maximize the effectiveness of focus group research. Chapter 3 discusses the focus group process from the time a project is conceived until the moderator's final report is presented. The emphasis is on actions that the client and moderator can take at each stage to insure that the client gets the maximum from the focus group project. This chapter emphasizes the *process* of focus groups, suggesting that clients should follow a well-defined series of steps in order to get the most from the research implemented.

2. Common mistakes made in focus group research. Chapter 4 has been included at the request of various organizations with whom I have talked about focus groups in recent years. Whenever I am planning to give a seminar or speech about focus groups, the topic that is almost always requested is the errors researchers make in focus groups. This chapter identifies the most common mistakes. By learning from mistakes that have been made by others, it will be much easier for moderators to avoid making them in the future.

3. The focus group moderator. Chapter 5 discusses the role of the moderator in the focus group industry at the current time and the relationship this person should have with the client. It analyzes what client organizations should expect from moderators through-

out the process, and how a client organziation can—and should—evaluate the performances of the moderators they retain.

4. The escalating costs of focus group research. One of the biggest issues in the market research industry at the present time is the rise in absolute costs of focus groups—they have almost doubled in the last five or seven years. Chapter 6 discusses the factors that go into the cost of focus group research and suggests ways that the costs can be significantly reduced.

5. Modern focus group moderating techniques. Chapter 7 provides an in-depth discussion of several new moderation techniques that have been developed to increase the depth and quality of information generated from focus groups. This chapter gives specific examples of the use of different techniques in actual research situations. By reading this chapter, moderators should be able to use some of these approaches in future groups.

6. Trends in the 1990s. This chapter 9 takes a look into the future of the focus group industry and makes predictions as to where it will be heading over the next decade.

7. A career in focus groups. Chapter 11 discusses some of the career opportunities that exist in the focus group industry for someone who is interested in becoming a moderator. Covered in this chapter are topics like how to get into the industry and where to get trained. Chapter 12 provides helpful suggestions on building a focus group research moderation business.

8. The focus group research facility. Chapter 13 discusses the vital role of the research facility in focus group research and suggests actions that should be taken to strengthen this link in the research chain. The proposals raised in this chapter assign the facility a different and much greater degree of responsibility for their role in successful research than they have had in the past.

I would like to think that this is the last book I will write about focus groups. But if the experience of the past few years is at all indicative of the future, another book will be needed in the mid-1990s.

Until that time, I hope this book will be interesting and helpful to both moderators and clients in producing more effective focus group research.

Acknowledgments

Many people have been extremely helpful to me in the preparation of this second book on focus group research. Perhaps most important have been the readers of my first book, *The Practical Handbook and Guide to Focus Group Research*. Hundreds of them told me how helpful that book was to them, and they are my principal motivation for writing this one. I certainly hope that this book adds to their knowledge of focus groups and helps them as research practitioners, as client users of focus group research, or in any other capacity, to increase their knowledge of market research methodologies.

I also want to express appreciation to my wife—and best friend—who has put up with my hyper energy level for almost thirty years. I have always received the greatest encouragement from Rosalie for the mission I have established for myself, to share my thoughts about focus groups. Without her support throughout the process, this book would never have been written.

Elaine Shepherd, my secretary and administrative assistant since I started in the consulting business in 1973, must be acknowledged not only in this book but in almost everything else I do. We have worked together as a team for many years, and my successes would never have happened without her. She is the consummate professional and has contributed to my literary efforts in more ways than she will ever know.

I also want to acknowledge the contribution of Roy Bostock to this book, and I am honored that he would lend his name and kind comments to it. I have known Roy for twenty-five years, going back to my days at Procter & Gamble, when he was the account supervisor over Charmin Toilet Tissue at Benton & Bowles. I had great respect and admiration for him at that time and have enjoyed watching his career blossom over the ensuing years. I feel particularly lucky that our careers came together again when we sold Connecticut Consulting Group to DMB&B, permitting me to work with him once again.

I also want to thank Dave Quincy, an executive vice-president at Clarion and one of the smartest and most capable people I have ever met. Dave introduced me to the world of industrial focus groups and has taught me more about that segment of American business than I ever thought possible. Without his help, support, and counsel, I would never have seen the possibility of translating market research methodologies to industries like electronic controls, computers, factory automation, and voice and data wiring devices. I am a better person today, and a much more qualified focus group moderator, because I spent so much time working with Dave over the past several years.

I would also like to acknowledge the assistance of Susan Weiss and the people at Focus First America in Stamford, Connecticut. This is one of the premier focus group facilities in the United States and is a prototype for an effective research facility. I have appreciated the inputs of Susan and her staff over the years, and I have learned more about the operations of facilities from Susan than from anyone else.

I also want to recognize and appreciate the input of Warren Goldman, the owner of New York Conference Center and a colleague in the focus group moderator business. Warren, a real pro, is always willing to share his knowledge with other practitioners. For this I have great respect and admiration, and I could not have written some of the parts of this book without his advice and counsel.

Finally, I want to acknowledge all the special clients I have had over the past several years. You know who you are, as we have worked closely together on many projects and wrestled with issues both easy and difficult. A professional in any service industry is only as good as the clients with whom he or she works. I have been blessed with unusually rewarding clients, not only in the organizations they represent but in the people they are. I have made many good friends in my travels throughout the country doing focus groups on everything from automation to computers to magazines to skin care. All of you have made these efforts worthwhile and have allowed me to develop the inputs that made this book possible.

1

Focus Groups: An Overview

Because of the popularity of focus groups as a research technique, the term *focus groups* has come to mean different things to different people. In fact, today there are at least three different types of qualitative research that researchers utilize, all of which are called "focus groups." This chapter provides an overview of the focus group research methodology. Its purpose is to:

- describe the three major types of "focus groups" and identify the marketing applications for which each is generally employed;
- distinguish focus groups from other popular forms of qualitative research by defining each and explaining the most common applications and situations where each is used; and
- review the most common uses and abuses of the focus group technique.

Types of Focus Groups

Most people who do qualitative research would classify focus groups into three different types: *full groups, minigroups,* and *telephone groups.* All these have some elements in common, but there are also areas of significant differences among them. To understand their similarities and differences, and ultimately the reason why each technique is used, it is helpful to briefly define of each type.

- *Full group*—A full group consists of a discussion of approximately 90 to 120 minutes, led by a trained moderator, involving eight to ten persons who are recruited for the session based on their common demographics, attitudes, or buying patterns germane to the topic.

- *Minigroup*—A mini group is essentially the same as a full group, except that it generally contains four to six persons.
- *Telephone group*—In a telephone group, individuals participate in a telephone conference call, wherein they are led by a trained moderator for thirty minutes to two hours. They are recruited according to the same parameters as full and minigroups.

Similarities

The similarities among these three types of groups are important for understanding the technique and for deciding when each should be used. One similarity is that in all three group types, a trained moderator conducts the session. This person functions as the leader of the discussion and stimulates discussion among the participants, saying as little as possible during the group. The moderator does *not* operate like an interviewer in a quantitative or survey research situation, asking questions of the participants. Rather, he or she uses an outline or guide that has been prepared in advance by the moderator and/or client, based on the research objectives, and seeks to have the participants do most of the talking based on the probes in the guide.

Another similarity is that for all three focus group types, a reasonably homogeneous group of participants is selected, based on specific criteria, depending on the needs of the client organization. The objective is to configure the groups with persons who are capable of providing the highest-quality discussion about the topic being researched. Participants are paid for their involvement in the groups in amounts that vary dramatically according to how much incentive is necessary to motivate them to come to the sessions. It is possible to conduct focus groups without any payment to the participants, but only in a very small percentage of all focus groups can this be done. Interestingly, focus groups are the only popular market research technique in which participants are paid.

Finally, all three types of groups are audiotaped, to preserve a permanent record of the proceedings. A large percentage of full groups and minigroups are videotaped as well.

Differences

The differences among the various types of focus groups are integral to a thorough understanding of each.

Number of Participants. The biggest difference between full groups and minigroups is the number of participants involved. Full groups contain eight to ten people, whereas minigroups are limited to four or six. Some researchers prefer to use minigroups to full groups because they feel they can gain more in-depth information from a smaller group. The reason is that a group session lasts approximately 100 minutes; if ten people are involved, the average individual gets only ten minutes to participate. With the minigroup, the time per person is doubled, thus (theoretically) enabling the moderator to get more information from each individual.

Other researchers use minigroups because they find that it is not feasible to recruit more than six persons for a particular group. The small size of the qualified participant universe, the cost of obtaining subjects, or the general unwillingness of some target groups to be involved in focus group research are factors that may limit the feasibility of larger groups. This is not uncommon with medical focus groups or with groups of high-level executives of specialized businesses.

Telephone Groups. The differences between telephone groups and the other types are even more significant. Telephone groups are conducted in a conference call environment, and the participants and the moderator are all in different locations. By contrast, minigroups and full groups are almost always conducted in a special research facility, with all the participants interacting in the same room. Such facilities normally include a focus group room, with a large conference table around which the people sit during the discussion. Most also have an observation room connected to the focus group room by a one-way mirror so that client personnel can observe—and listen to—the session.

Telephone groups also offer more anonymity than either full or minigroups. They allow only limited interaction among the participants, due to the absence of face-to-face contact.

The moderator in a telephone group functions more like an interviewer than a discussion leader, due to the fact that the interaction among the participants is much more difficult to obtain than in a mini or full group. Telephone groups are normally much shorter than the other forms of focus groups; the average is an hour versus an hour and a half to two hours for traditional groups. Finally, it is very common for minigroups and full groups to be videotaped, so that the client organization can provide a record of the proceedings more complete than audiotape for people who were unable to attend the session. This is obviously impossible with a telephone group.

There are nonetheless several reasons why organizations often choose to use a telephone focus group instead a full or minigroup. Sometimes anonymity is critical in being able to recruit participants. If one wishes to conduct research to ascertain attitudes toward Product X among merchandising managers in different food chains, for example, the telephone group might be preferred. The merchandising managers may not be willing to share their views with their competitors in the room, but in an anonymous situation they might participate. The telephone approach provides the greatest anonymity of any type of focus group.

In other situations, qualified participants are not located near one another, so they must all be brought to one central location, usually at considerable expense. Therefore, the best way conduct research with them would be via a telephone conference call.

Finally, a telephone conference call is usually significantly less costly than a full or minigroup session. Participants are often not paid for their involvement, because the client organization does not have to travel to a central location to observe the proceedings, and because the costs of a telephone hookup are much less than those associated with renting a facility and feeding participants and client personnel.

Other Types of Qualitative Research

Focus groups are only one qualitative research technique. While focus groups are used significantly more frequently than any other type of qualitative research, it is essential for both moderators and clients to have a basic understanding of the other types and when each is most appropriate. Many organizations that face research situations immediately assume that they need a focus group. But there are situations where focus groups are *not* the best qualitative research techniques to use to obtain the information needed. Experienced researchers are trained to ask clients the right questions in the planning stages of a research effort in order to determine the most efficient and cost effective approach to achieve the research objectives.

This section briefly reviews the most common types of qualitative research that should be considered. It is important to recognize that *qualitative* research itself is often not the best methodology to meet the informational needs that have been raised, and that a quantitative methodology may be more appropriate. (This book will not address quantitative research methods, as that subject was covered in great detail in *the Practical Handbook and Guide to Focus Group Research.*)

There are essentially three major types of qualitative research besides focus groups. This section defines each one and gives examples of situations in which their use would be appropriate.

One-on-Ones

One-on-ones, also known as in-depth interviews (IDIs), involve a discussion between a trained moderator and a qualified respondent, who has been selected by criteria of interest to the client organization, about a specific topic. One-on-ones vary in length from a half hour to one and one-half hours, with the average being approximately forty-five minutes.

As in a focus group, a detailed moderator guide is normally developed for one-on-ones. One-on-ones are generally conducted in a research facility that contains a one-way mirror so the client can observe the proceedings.

A researcher may consider a one-on-one to be the preferable research technique for several reasons.

- The research topic is highly personal and not conducive to discussion in a group environment, such as the participant's sexual behavior, personal finances, or drug or alcohol usage.
- A participant is inhibited from talking in a group due to a competitive situation. Some companies prohibit their employees from participating in focus groups but allow them to be interviewed in a one-on-one session for this reason.
- The product category is highly complex, and additional time

is needed to ensure that the participant understands the question.

- A one-on-one may provide significantly more in-depth information than is possible with other forms of qualitative research, because of the concentrated time spent on the topic with each participant.

Although most researchers agree that there are situations where one-on-ones are preferable, this research technique also has some important disadvantages. These include:

- The cost per interview is significantly more expensive than a focus group, as the costs of the moderator and the facility are amortized over only one person, versus the eight or ten in a focus group.
- One-on-ones are much more time consuming, if input is to be gained from a reasonable number of people (ten to twenty). This can be a major issue with the client, as few people are willing remain at a facility to observe ten or twenty hours of interviews. By contrast, it is generally not difficult to motivate people to watch one or two focus group sessions.
- One-on-one interviews are much more difficult to interpret than focus groups, due to the sequential (as opposed to simultaneous) receipt of information about each element of the moderator guide. In a focus group, all ten people will provide their views on a particular topic (within the guide) within a concentrated period of time. On the other hand, in a one-on-one the input is often spread out over several days, thus making it more difficult to assimilate the information and try to develop a sense of the consensus.
- The one-on-one technique does not enable the moderator to leverage the benefits of peer interaction that exist in focus groups. Many researchers feel that one of the most valuable benefits of focus groups is the dynamics of the discussion that occurs among the participants.

Dyads

The second form of qualitative research is the dyad, which is quite similar to the one-on-one except that there are two participants present with the moderator. The dyad is not a commonly used research technique, as most researchers prefer either the one-on-one or a type of focus group. But sometimes a dyad represents a more effective technique than the alternatives, especially in situations where two people are relatively equal partners in a decision-making process but have somewhat conflicting views on the topic.

A life insurance company, for example, might prefer to use dyads to gather consumer input about its product, because husbands and wives often have very different views on the value of life insurance. The husband's objectives may be to purchase life insurance to protect his family in the event of his death (and therefore loss of income) but to spend as little as possible for this coverage since it will never have a direct benefit to him. Further, the more money he spends on life insurance, the less he has now to spend on things of interest to him. Therefore, his reaction might be to purchase a less expensive policy (like a term insurance policy) or to buy less life insurance than might be needed, in order to keep the costs at the lowest possible level. Because of this common orientation, research conducted with men only might point to developing a strategy of selling life insurance under a "value for your money" positioning, or to focusing the attention of the sales and marketing communications activities on term insurance.

On the other hand, if the person interviewed is the beneficiary (presumably the wife), the conclusions of the research might be very different. The wife may be much less concerned with immediate cash-flow issues in order to gain the protection she will need in the future. To this end, she may feel a need to purchase larger amounts of insurance than would her husband. She may also prefer permanent life insurance to term insurance due to the value she perceives of the cash value buildup, borrowing capabilities, and rate protection as her insured husband gets older. As a result of the wife's perspective, a marketing program based on discussions with women alone might stress the investment nature of permanent life insurance and the need for large amounts of coverage in order to provide protection for a family in the event of the husband's death. This approach might also add disability insurance to the policy, since the need for protection might be considerable in the event the primary wage earner (in this case, the man) cannot work.

Such differences in opinion about life insurance can be handled very effectively in a dyad, where the moderator has both the husband and wife in the room. The moderator can then direct the discussion so as to benefit from the inputs of both parties. In this type of research the moderator can determine the views of both "decision influencers," as well as assess the relative importance of the various issues to both parties, so that the marketing and communications programs developed subsequently reflect the needs of both parties. The dyad technique may be the only way to achieve such an objective when two people are so important in a decision-making process.

Another example of the value of a dyad is a situation where an equipment manufacturer is seeking to gain input about a new machine from a target customer—say, a Fortune 500 company. If the research is conducted only with the plant manager (that is, the person responsible for managing the equipment), the researchers might get a very different view of the requirements of the equipment than if they talked to the comptroller, who is primarily interested in the cost implications of the equipment. In a situation like this, where two key people are integral to the product purchase decision, a dyad is a very effective way to gather inputs from them.

In summary, dyads can be very effective if used selectively. They have the same problems (and to some degree the same benefits) as one-on-ones, and therefore they have a place in some research programs. It is important to be aware of this technique, so that when the need arises, the researcher is in a position to evaluate the viability of a dyad to meet the client's needs.

Small-Scale Quantitative

Paradoxically, the third form of qualitative research involves the application of traditional *quantitative* research methodologies (such as telephone, personal, and mailed surveys) but it utilizes samples that are small in size, for directional purposes only, and not therefore do not have statistical reliability.

Suppose the client is a leading brandy manufacturer that is interested in getting information about the attitudes of liquor store owners toward a specific promotional program they are planning. One approach would be to implement an extensive quantitative research study involving several hundred respondents randomly selected from the total universe of chain and independent liquor stores. The information the client would get from this study would have statistical reliability, so they should be able to project the results to all liquor store owners. But the brandy manufacturer does not want to go to the expense or trouble of implementing such an extensive study, yet they still would like some directional input on their promotional program. They do have the option of using qualitative research techniques. If they decide that a one-on-one dyad, or focus group is not appropriate, a good alternative for them is the small-scale quantitative study. Such a study would involve twenty to thirty respondents, all of whom would be administered a "quantitative" research questionnaire as if they were part of a large study (with a sample of 300 to 400 respondents). Since the size of the sample is so small, however, it is not possible to project the results to all liquor store owners. So the client should consider the output to be a *qualitative* research effort.

Small-scale quantitative research is used in a great variety of ways by marketing and product development people to study a variety of topics. The different reasons why a researcher might use small-scale quantitative research rather than another form of qualitative research are several.

- Small-scale studies are generally much less expensive than focus groups and one-on-ones.
- Many people feel that they can obtain more data by executing a detailed quantitative questionnaire among a small sample than by implementing one of the other forms of qualitative research.
- Other factors associated with the research might suggest that a small-scale qualitative study would be the most effective and efficient research technique to use. For example, the target customers for the research may not be easily accessible because they are geographically dispersed.
- Sometimes a small-scale quantitative study is used in order to pretest a questionnaire intended for a larger quantitative study. The objective here would be to learn whether the questionnaire is worded so that the respondents can easily understand all elements of it. Other reasons for using small-scale quantitative research are to determine the length of the interview that the questionnaire requires and the effectiveness of the skip pattern that has been developed in the question sequencing. For such cases, small-scale quantitative research may be the best approach.

In summary, small-scale quantitative research is another qualitative technique that may be appropriate in various research projects.

The Uses of Focus Group Research

There are essentially nine different uses of the focus group technique. This section describes each and provides specific examples of the types of research questions that I have seen used for each of the approaches. I believe that all "appropriate" uses of focus group research fall into one of the following categories:

New Product Development Studies. One of the most common uses of focus groups, new product development covers a wide range of subject matter. The most frequent use of focus groups in this area is to expose a new product concept or prototype to a group of consumers to obtain their reactions, in order to identify the strengths and weaknesses of the concept. The product development team modifies the concept or prototype based on the inputs received, then conduct additional qualitative or quantitative research to assess consumer reaction to the modified version.

Positioning Studies. Positioning studies are often thought of as strategic focus groups, since their purpose is to identify the most effective way to communicate to target consumers about a particular product, service, or institution. When a large financial service organization, for example, was seeking to change its image with its target consumers, focus groups were an integral part of its overall image development program. Specifically, we used focus groups to help identify the strengths and weaknesses of the current image, then to obtain participants' reactions to several new positioning directions. By analyzing the participants' responses to the new approaches, we were able to develop an overall corporate positioning that leveraged the existing strengths of the organization and that communicated a message that was meaningful to the target consumers relative to their desires and expectations.

Positioning focus groups are also used frequently to help advertisers find the most appropriate way to talk about individual products or services, so that they communicate a unique and meaningful message to the target consumers. This process first assesses the current image of the product or service, then exposes several prototype positioning alternatives to the participants in order to ascertain the strengths and weaknesses of each alternative.

Habits and Usage Studies. In habits and usage studies, focus group research is employed to obtain basic information from participants about their usage of different products or services. A bank seeking to develop a program to increase usage of its ATM machines, for example, might conduct focus groups with both users and nonusers to determine such things as how often they use ATM machines and tellers, respectively; their principal reasons for using or not using ATM machines; their key problems with ATM machines; and the factors that would motivate them to use ATM machines more often.

A habits and usage focus group is most likely to be employed when a client needs quantitative research about consumer usage patterns and wishes to collect preliminary data to help understand how consumers utilize the product or service. These groups are very commonly used in advertising agencies to help account personnel learn more about businesses with which they are not familiar, so that they can develop more effective presentations to win new accounts.

Packaging Assessments. Focus groups are often used to obtain consumer reactions to new packaging, whether it is in the conceptual and rough art stage or in relatively final form. In the early stages, the objective of the focus group is normally to identify the strengths and weaknesses of various packaging elements. The designers can then modify those elements as the program moves to the prototype stage. Packaging research is also used at this stage to help copywriters develop the package copy that is most effective in terms of memorability, believability, and visibility to the consumer.

When focus groups are employed in later (or comp) stages of package design, their principal purpose is often a "disaster check," to insure that no elements of the packaging are offensive to the consumer or have connotations inconsistent with the product's image or positioning.

Packaging focus groups are often followed up with quantitative research, which is generally necessary to obtain the information the client needs to make substantive decisions on package design.

Attitude Studies. A large percentage of focus groups are conducted to collect information about how target consumers feel about different products, services, and programs. The publisher of a new magazine, for example, might conduct groups to identify how the readers feel about it, both in its own right and compared with the other magazines they read. This information would enable the editorial staff to make changes in the publication to reflect the readers' interests, so that future issues would gain a more positive response.

An attitude study could also be conducted by a new retail store seeking patrons' reactions to such things as product selection, store design, service, and so on. One of the most popular forms of attitude research is aimed at service quality evaluations. Such studies ask consumers how well the client company provides them with customer service in areas such as the employees' responsiveness, courtesy, knowledgeability, accessibility, and so on. Attitude studies are used very frequently by public relations agencies to determine consumer attitudes toward specific issues, so they can design more effective publicity programs to achieve the objectives of their clients.

Advertising/Copy Evaluations. Focus groups are commonly used to provide input to advertising agencies and client companies (advertisers) about the effectiveness of their advertising executions. This can be done during the creative development stage, at which point consumers are exposed to rough ideas using a storyboard; in the layout phase, to get inputs before making final recommendations; or in the postadvertising phase, when consumers are asked for their feelings about an advertising campaign that has been under way for some time. Focus groups can also be a very important element in advertising copy development programs, as long as the objective of the group is to secure inputs about consumer attitudes toward the advertising rather than to determine whether the advertising has succeeded in generating consumer recall—a task that only quantitative research can do effectively.

Promotion Evaluations. Focus groups are used extensively not only in the development stages of a consumer and trade promotion program but also in the postevent assessment, to determine the relative effectiveness of the event. Like a successful advertising campaign, the creation of an effective promotional program requires consumer inputs, and focus groups are often the most effective way to secure them. Specifically, groups are used to obtain consumer reactions to promotion concepts, so that the ideas can later be refined and made more interesting, more appealing, or easier to understand. After an event is completed, focus groups are often employed to gain consumer reactions to it and to learn why they did or did not participate in the event.

Idea Generation. Focus groups are occasionally used by organizations to stimulate new ideas. Such groups are structured to get the participants to talk about problems they are having with a particular task or about the unfulfilled needs they have in a product category. This way, the client can identify specific areas where new products—or modifications in existing ones—might offer benefits. It is important to remember that participants cannot be expected to *create* new ideas and new products. They can talk about the problems they are having and the wishes they would like to have fulfilled, but they will not normally be the source of new ideas. These have to come from the client's or moderator's interpretation of their comments.

Employee Attitude and Motivation Studies. Finally, focus groups are used to assess corporate employees's attitudes toward their organization. Personnel departments often use them to gain a feeling for the morale in their company and to identify any problems among the employees that should be addressed.

The Abuses of Focus Groups

Because of the popularity of focus groups, many organizations have used them as a panacea for solving their informational needs. Whenever a question comes up, some people feel that the only way to answer it is to conduct a focus group. While focus groups are an excellent research methodology that can provide valuable information in very many situations, the technique is frequently used improperly, in situations where a different technique would be more appropriate in light of the company's research objectives. This section identifies the most common ways that companies use focus group research incorrectly. It is my feeling that marketers who are aware of these abuses will be discouraged from using focus groups to accomplish research objectives that are not consistent with the technique's capabilities.

Abuse 1: Using Focus Groups as a Cheap Alternative to Quantitative Research. This is a very common mistake that organizations make, particularly in recessionary periods when research budgets are tight. Instead of implementing a $40,000 quantitative study to assess usage patterns and attitudes, for example, an organization may choose to implement two focus groups on the topic—at a cost of about 20 percent of the quantitative survey. The company then seeks to make decisions based on *qualitative* discussions among twenty people that should be based on *quantitative* interviews with four hundred. The results are likely to be misleading and could ultimately damage the overall marketing program.

Abuse 2: Using Focus Groups to Produce Data That They Are Not Intended to Generate. While focus groups can be used to obtain many kinds of information, there are some things that they cannot do effectively. They cannot be appropriately used to:

- estimate sales from a new product or service;
- determine the level of advertising recall that an ad campaign has generated or will create;
- project repeat purchase patterns among those who try a new product or service;
- determine which packaging alternative will work best for a product line;
- determine the optimal price of a product or service.

Abuse 3: Implementing More Focus Groups Than Are Necessary to Achieve the Research Objectives. Some researchers and client organizations ignore the fact that focus group research is *qualitative* and as such does not provide projectable data. But some clients seek to compensate for this disadvantage by holding many groups, often ten to fifteen groups on a particular topic. Their reasoning is that since data from focus groups are not meaningful if only a few sessions are implemented, the number of groups in the series should be increased. In reality, this probably does little to improve the projectability of the data (since the data are still *qualitative*), but it does make some people feel better.

Abuse 4: Conducting Groups in Different Locations Unnecessarily. In one of the most common focus group abuses, researchers feel that they must have diverse geographical representation in their research program. Therefore they conduct groups in several different markets, then feel confident that their survey has adequately represented the entire country. My experience suggests that in reality, focus groups normally do not have to be conducted in more than one or two markets, as differences rarely emerge as a result of geographical considerations. So unless a client has a concrete reason to believe that there are real differences in attitudes toward or usage of their product or service across different markets, focus groups should be limited to as few cities as possible. Internal "political" considerations are often the driving force in expanding focus group research to multiple cities, to meet the self-interest of different constituencies.

Abuse 5: Taking the Focus Group Technique Insufficiently Seriously. Due to the qualitative nature of focus group research, some clients approach focus groups very informally. This can dramatically affect the quality of the output from the research. Specifically:

- Their advance preparations are inadequate. The moderator is improperly briefed; the correct participants are not recruited; an effective moderator guide is not developed; or the most appropriate external stimuli to secure the maximum quality from the participants have not been selected.
- They are not selective about the moderator, even though the moderator is the most important element in focus group research.
- They do not attend the groups themselves, or they do not pay attention when they are behind the mirror. Some clients spend more time talking and joking behind the mirror than they do observing the group and figuring out the implications.

Abuse 6: Taking the Focus Group Technique Too Seriously. Clients and moderators must always keep in mind that the focus group technique is *qualitative* and that the input from any single participant in the group is relatively unimportant. Some client observers focus their attention on the comments of only one or two participants and assume that their view is the consensus view of the entire group. The key to the effective use of focus groups, by contrast, is to identify the overall sense of the group relative to the idea being discussed, not to focus on the input of any individual.

Summary

Qualitative research encompasses several different techniques, each of which has inherent strengths and weaknesses. Focus groups are one important technique among them. When used appropriately, focus groups can be extremely effective in generating meaningful information about consumer attitudes toward a variety of different topics. It is important point to establish research objectives early in the process so that the most appropriate technique can be chosen to meet them.

Qualitative Research Outline

Types of Focus Groups
    Full group—eight to ten persons
    Minigroup—four to six persons
    Telephone group—using conference call
      Anonymity
      Geographical location
Other Types of Qualitative Research
    One-on-ones
      Advantages
        Useful when topic is not conducive to group discussion
        Useful when participants are competitors
      Disadvantages
        Require more explanation
        More time-consuming
        Costlier
        Harder to interpret
        No group interaction

Dyads
  Useful when there are two decision-influencers
Small-scale quantitative
  Advantages
    Cost
    Geographic dispersal
    Pretesting
Uses of Focus Group Research
  New product development studies
  Positioning studies
  Habits and usage studies
  Packaging assessments
  Attitude studies
  Advertising/copy evaluations
  Promotion evaluations
  Idea generation
  Employee attitude and motivation studies
Abuses of Focus Groups
  As a cheap alternative to quantitative research
  To generate data that they are not intended to generate
  Implementing more than are necessary
  Using different locations unnecessarily
  Taking the technique insufficiently seriously
  Taking the technique too seriously

2

Research Decisions

One of the most important decisions that marketing professionals are regularly asked to make involves whether to research, and if so, what kind of research to conduct. This chapter suggests some guidelines for deciding whether to conduct research and what kind. Specifically:

- Should an organization research the issue under consideration?
- If so, should the research methodology be quantitative or qualitative—or a mixture of the two?
- Should the organization do the research itself, or hire an outsider to conduct it?

Deciding Whether to Research

Deciding whether to conduct market research to address a particular question is something that many organizations find to be extremely difficult and quite time-consuming. In most situations, the principal reason why making a research decision becomes difficult is because the thinking regarding the proposed research is often focused on *executional* rather than on *strategic* issues. Executional issues involve such things as:

- Determining where the funding for the research will come from, and how it will be allocated if more than one department, division, or product group stands to benefit from the outcome of the research.
- Determining whether the research employed should be

qualitative or quantitative and, within these broad classifications, what the best methodology to answer the research question would be. While these are important issues that need to be discussed in great detail in planning the research project, they should *not* be a part of the basic decision on whether to utilize research.

* Determining the geographic areas where the research will be conducted and defining the target audience to be interviewed and the size of the sample to be employed. Again, these are all very important decisions that have to be made, but none of them should be a consideration relative to the basic decision on whether to conduct research.

In essence, *executional issues are those that deal with the implementation of a research study that is already being planned,* whereas the *strategic issues involve whether it is in the best interest of an organization to conduct this research* at all.

There are four key factors that should influence the decision on whether to implement a proposed research study. All of them should be addressed by the client organization before it agrees to implement any parts of a research program. These are the *strategic* issues involved in the research decision.

Strategic Issue 1: Will the Cost of Doing the Research Exceed the Value of the Information?

In any situation where research is being contemplated, this is the first and most important question that must be addressed. Research inputs, like most elements of the marketing mix, have an economic value that must be one of the decision criteria. For example, if an insurance company is offering a new service, it has basically two alternatives.

Conducting Research to Determine the Reaction of the Target Consumers to the New Service. In this case, the insurance company might develop a prototype description of the new service, or even mock up the materials that would be used to sell it, and expose this information to consumers. Depending on the type of research it implements, the company could gather inputs such as:

- Consumers' overall reaction to the service, both in the absolute and compared with similar offerings of competitors.
- The strengths and weaknesses of the service, including the elements that are particularly appealing and the limitations that consumers see in it as it is now.
- Consumers' intentions to purchase the service. Depending on the research methodology employed and the overall budget allocated to it, the insurance company might be able to develop a computer model to project what the value of the service would be if it were introduced broadly across the United States.

Introducing the Service Without Conducting Any Research and Judging Its Success by the Reaction to It in the Actual Marketplace. There are no research costs in this approach; but the service is introduced without the benefit of consumer input, which is very risky. The approach's success depends on the judgment of the people who have developed the service and their ability to anticipate the needs and desires of the target market.

Researching a new product or service can itself be thought of as a kind of insurance for a client, and spending money on research before introducing a new product is much like buying insurance. The more research is conducted, the greater the chances that the new product will succeed in the marketplace. If the insurance company feels very confident about its new service, going directly to market without the benefit of research may be acceptable. But if it is eager to increase the chances of success of the new service, research would be appropriate, as the service could be modified prior to introduction based on the research.

It is often helpful to consider the advantages of each of these two options for a new product or service. Weighing the advantages of each provides a very important input into the insurance company's decision to research or not to research its new service.

The Advantages of the No-Research Approach:

- The new service will be introduced on a faster timetable. It will provide incremental revenues more quickly than would be the case with a delayed entry. Quicker entry protects the idea from being copied or preempted by an industry competitor.

- The ultimate volume and profit potential of the new service will be available to the insurance company much sooner, since actual "sales" results are immediately obtained.
- Information about consumer acceptance of the new service will be more accurate than information that comes from any research option. Thus, the insurance company will know whether the new service is successful, although it will have very little information as to why. This might not be critical in the case of a clear failure or an outright success. But if the service introduction fails by a small margin, the insurance company will not know what the strengths and weaknesses are of the service are in order to improve it in the future.

The Advantages of the Research Approach:

- The insurance company can test all the different elements of the new service package, with target consumers in order to identify its strengths and weaknesses and the areas of confusion. As a result, the company will be able to modify the elements of the new service to minimize its weak points and emphasize the strengths.
- The insurance company will go into the market with a stronger overall program than if no research had been conducted. Going to the marketplace with its "best foot forward" increases the probability of success with the new service.

Strategic Issue 2: Is There Enough Time to do Research?

In some situations, timing is the crucial issue in deciding whether to conduct research. Time can be important in situations like these:

- *The product is seasonal.* A seasonal product or service must be introduced at a particular time, or a full year may be lost. Examples are a new barbecue sauce, a new swimwear line, a new lawn-care product, or a new type of snow glove.
- *The product is a fad product.* For a fad product such as a

tie-in with a hot movie, rock group, or television character, timing is key. Most of these types of products need to be introduced on an opportunistic basis, since the time it would take to research them could consume a considerable portion of their total life cycle.

- *The product can easily be copied by a competitor and only the first to market will be successful.* In this case, the decision to introduce without research might be very prudent.

On the other hand, there are situations where it is better to be a laggard into the market. When other companies have introduced a similar product or service, the client product or service can be developed based on knowledge of consumer reactions from the marketplace.

Strategic Issue 3: Is Research Capable of Providing the Information that is Needed?

A very important consideration in the strategic thinking about any research program is the very possibility of obtaining answers from research. This is normally a function of two factors:

- Are the participants in the research *capable* of answering the questions desired of them, in such a way that will provide reliable results? For example, many advertisers use research to determine which of several different media that they have used has had the greatest impact on target consumers. To obtain this information, research questionnaires are used that ask respondents where they have seen the client advertising message. Unfortunately, the answers to this question normally do not reflect reality, since people relate much more to the content of advertising messages than to the vehicle that delivers them. When questioned, consumers tend to name the broadcast media (television particularly, but also radio) most often as the place they say they saw or heard a message, even if the company did not advertise over television or radio.
- Are the consumers *willing* to provide the desired information? Organizations that conduct research in the

financial services industry, for example, find this to be a particularly important issue, as it is often quite difficult to obtain accurate inputs about personal income, savings, investing, and spending. These are areas where many people tend to refuse to share information with researchers, or prefer to lie so that they seem more affluent than they really are.

People's willingness to answer questions also becomes an issue in personal questions about toilet habits, sexual behavior, religious feelings, personal hygiene, and the like. These are very sensitive topics for many people, and results from research questionnaires about them tend not to be particularly accurate. In fact, the nonresponse rate (that is, refusal to answer) for these types of questions frequently is dramatically higher than that for less personal topics.

Strategic Issue 4: Will the Results of the Research be Believed and Acted Upon?

This is often the most important strategic issue in deciding whether to do research. Many companies use research for the purpose of confirming their previously held beliefs, and if the results do not agree with them, the research is discarded.

In fact, one of the biggest problems that qualitative researchers have with some of their clients is the "kill the messenger" syndrome. Suppose that a researcher exposes a new concept to target consumers, and they do not receive the idea well. The company that hired the researcher will often blame the researcher. If the researcher used a focus group, the client may blame the moderator for not properly presenting the idea to the group. If the researcher used a quantitative questionnaire, the company may blame the people who developed the questionnaire for not asking the right questions. Another rationalization that client companies make is to decide that the wrong target audience has been researched, and that if the concept were shown to a different set of people, the response would be very different. While these kinds of situations do happen, most often the idea itself was not sound in the first place.

If the client organization is not willing to accept the results of the research for the overall decision-making process, then the study being considered should not be conducted. One way to avoid the client's rejection of the results is to gain the client's consent to each part of the research. Every question asked must adhere to the client's standards of believability or usability, or it will not be meaningful to ask it. Therefore, before any research questionnaire is used, the researcher must test its validity to ensure that the client organization will accept whatever results are achieved rather than consider the results only if they confirm the client's own preconception.

Deciding on Qualitative or Quantitative Research

Once the decision to research has been made, the next key decision concerns the type of research that should be executed, considering the broad spectrum of quantitative and qualitative research methodologies. The general type of research needs to be decided before the actual technique is determined. Many different factors influence the decision on which type of research methodology to employ; qualitative, quantitative, or a combination of the two. This section identifies the most important issues to consider in planning a research program, *after* the decision has been made to undertake one.

Budget

In many cases, the most important factor that affects the type of research selected is the amount of money available to fund the research. Most commonly, the client organization identifies a need for specific information to be generated by research. The client then presents a budget to a researcher with the directive to develop the best possible approach that meets the informational needs and stays within the budget parameters.

In another common approach, the client describes its informational needs and asks the researcher for a proposal on the best way to generate the data. Unfortunately, this approach gives the research too little budgetous guidance. It is possible to develop research programs for $20,000 and $200,000 that are intended to achieve the same overall objective. The key differences are in the scope of the studies and the accuracy of the data, both of which are a function of the budget. In financially tight times, organizations tend to prefer qualitative to quantitative research techniques, as the latter can provide some consumer inputs at a lower cost than is possible with most quantitative methodologies.

The chart in table 2–1 puts some perspective on the costs of conducting various types of research. The costs indicated are estimates only, and the actual costs for the various research approaches may differ by 30 to 40 percent from these amounts, based on the quality of the research supplier, the questionnaire length, the participant recruiting criteria, geographic areas, and the like.

Timing

The second factor that is extremely important in deciding which type of research to conduct is the amount of time available to conduct it. The total time required to conduct a *qualitative* research study is dramatically different from that needed for most *quantitative* methodologies. Most *qualitative* research can be completed (including a written report) within three to four weeks after approval is given for the study to proceed. The process can be even faster if the recruiting of participants is very basic (selecting participants who are for example, users of liquid laundry detergents or owners of certificates of deposit) and if no formal report is necessary.

TABLE 2–1

Costs of Various Market Research Studies (1992 Estimate*)

Study Type	Cost	Assumptions
Focus Group	$8,500	• two groups; consumers; average incidence
One-on-one	$6,500	• 10 interviews over 2 days; average incidence
Telephone interview	$21,500	• 300 sample; average incidence; simple study design: 15-minute questionnaire
Mailed questionnaire	$22,750	• 300 qualified; 5% response rate; no incentive
Mall intercept (personal interviews)	$16,000	• 300 sample; average incidence; simple study design

* For each study type, the cost estimate includes questionnaire and/or moderator guide preparation, project implementation, report development, and a formal presentation of the results.

The time necessary to complete a *quantitative* study varies considerably based on the methodology employed and the nature of the questionnaire. Some quantitative methodologies can provide information very quickly, notably syndicated telephone studies, which occur on a regular basis (weekly or biweekly). Indeed, their reason for being is that they can be completed within a week after approval is given. However, this type of study is the exception! Most quantitative research studies (conducted by telephone or mall intercept) require seven to ten weeks to complete and those conducted by mail generally take even longer, as much as ten to thirteen weeks. Because of the long lead time that most quantitative studies require, many client organizations prefer to use *qualitative* methodologies because they do not have time to wait for the results from a quantitative study.

Projectability

Some research studies have the objective of being able to project the attitudes or feelings of a sample population to the entire universe. For example, the study might compare consumer attitudes toward Product A and Product B; the level of consumer awareness of a particular advertising campaign; or the percentage of people in the United States who will buy a new product that has been introduced into a test market.

For a situation requiring research data that can be projected to a larger universe, the only option available to the researcher is *quantitative* research, since no qualitative methodologies can accurately project the results to the total population.

Direct Client Involvement

In some situations, it is important that the key persons from the client organization be an integral part of the research effort and actually experience participants reactions to the issue being evaluated. Such situations may include:

- Research conducted on reactions to an advertising concept. The copywriters will likely want to hear what the participants say about the concept. This gives the copywriters the inputs they need to further develop the advertising to achieve its intended objectives.

- Research involving new product concepts or prototypes. It is essential that the people in the product design and manufacturing areas hear the participants comments. That way, they can modify the design based on the reactions in order to build a product that has the best possible acceptance.

- The key decision makers have preconceived notions about consumer reactions to a product or service, and they need to be convinced that their perspectives are in correct or require significant modification. In such situations, it is often very advantageous to have the skeptics observe the focus groups, since participants' reactions to the product or service can influence their views more than most reports written by consultants or employees of the company.

If direct client involvement is viewed as necessary to the research project, qualitative research is the only viable option. In qualitative research the client can (and normally does) observe the proceedings from behind a one-way mirror. Further, the client can ensure that the flow of the discussion is consistent with the overall research objectives by interacting with the moderator a various times during the session. This enables the focus group process to be a two way interaction involving the client and the moderator, the moderator and the participants.

Use of the Research

The type of research selected often depends heavily on the intended use of the results of the study. If the results are to be used in a *development process,* a qualitative methodology is usually employed.

- To gain consumer input about a series of advertising ideas as part of a creative development effort, clients normally select qualitative methodologies.

- To learn how consumers feel about new packaging, a new promotion or a new product design, clients often select a qualitative approach, since the research will be used to help the design team improve the quality of the packaging, promotion, or design.

- To learn how consumers feel about a new product concept that is in the process of being developed, clients generally use qualitative methodologies. They need to gain the consumer information, make the modifications indicated, then quickly expose the modified idea to further groups to assess whether the changes are on target.

On the other hand, if the research is intended to provide a *picture of the market at a given point in time,* a quantitative methodology is more appropriate.

- A company that recently implemented an advertising campaign wants to find out how many people are aware of it, and what they remember about the creative content. A quantitative methodology will generally provide this client with more satisfactory results. It will indicate that that X percent of the target audience is aware of the advertising and that among them Y percent can recall one copy message and Z percent can recall the other. This type of study tells the client what the status of its advertising effort with consumers was at a point in time (that is, the period when the interview were held).
- A company has a new product in the market and wants to understand the penetration it has achieved. The best way to gather this type of information is with quantitative research. Using quantitative research, the company can determine the percentage of people who have purchased its product and the likelihood that others will buy it in the future.

Locale

In some situations, the locale of the study significantly affects the type of research chosen. A client seeking input from a sample that is representative of the entire United States must use some type of quantitative research, as it is impossible to get this breadth of representation with qualitative approaches. Also, if the people the client wants to study are located in very diverse locations, it could be forced to use a quantitative methodology, due to the high cost of reaching geographically dispersed people with qualitative approaches. It is inexpensive to implement a telephone or mail survey among a geographically dispersed group; but it is very costly (or logistically impossible) to have people in very remote areas come to one location to participate in a focus group or one-on-one interviews. It is also very expensive to send a trained moderator to conduct personal interviews or focus groups in remote locations.

Amount and Type of Information Desired

In some situations a client is seeking a great deal of information from the respondents. The only way the researcher can collect it all is to conduct the survey in the respondents' homes. For example, a client of mine sought to examine consumer use of batteries, specifically the size of and trends in the battery market, by chemical type (zinc carbon, alkaline, and mercury), battery size (AA, AAA, C, and D), and application (radio, flashlight, toy). For the study, my team asked the participants to inventory the batteries they used at home, so we could collect actual data rather than what the participants could remember. Such information can be obtained only by using quantitative methodologies.

What Type of Research to Use: Summary

The chart in table 2–2 summarizes the most important considerations in determining the type of research to conduct to achieve the research objectives.

Deciding Whether to Conduct Research In-House

Among organizations that need to obtain information through research, an important issue in recent years has been to decide whether they should conduct their own qualitative research or retain independent research consultants to do it. Some people feel that conducting focus groups and one-on-ones is relatively easy and can be handled with in-house personnel, thereby saving time and significant research dollars for the organization.

Doing it oneself is rarely considered when it comes to quantitative research, because of the widespread perception that expertise is needed to conduct a quantitative study (for example, to do sample selection, computer specifications, coding, interviewing, and training). A similar perception exists for many people about interview-

TABLE 2–2
Considerations for Research

Qualitative Research	Quantitative Research
Qualitative research is desirable when: • modifications need to be made in an idea before it is finalized • very fast consumer input is needed • the research budget is limited • client observation of the research is necessary • there is a need to probe deeply into the causes of some observed behavior.	Quantative research is desirable when: • a picture of the market at a given point in time is needed • data that can be projected to a larger universe are needed • the target participants for the research are geographically dispersed or difficult to reach • large amount of specific information from participants is sought • the data must be statistically representative of a very large geographic area.

ing techniques: Most marketing people recognize that it is likely to be a waste of time for them to try to conduct telephone or personal interviews for a quantitative study, if the firm is not staffed with qualified people to do this type of work in-house. Further, they understand that it does require training to be an effective interviewer, and that the "down time" of available employees cannot be used to conduct interviews.

But when it comes to focus groups and one-on-ones, the attitudes of many organizations are extremely different. Some corporate research persons feel they should do their own qualitative research rather than retain outside professionals. This section summarizes the principal arguments for and against doing your own qualitative research.

The Case for Doing Qualitative Research In-House

Cost Savings. There are significant cost savings in conducting focus groups or one-on-ones in-house since the company will not have to pay for an outside professional. Some organizations want to use the money saved to fund other research activities. The key question that needs to be addressed is whether the cost savings are worthwhile in the light of the better quality of the research that might result from using an independent, professional moderator.

Expertise. One of the biggest arguments in favor of conducting one's own focus groups is that a company knows more about its own product or service than almost any outsider and can therefore discuss it more knowledgeably with participants in focus groups or one-on-ones then an outside researcher can. Further, this knowledge of the product category enables the company observers to hear the nuances of the discussion, and therefore they are able to get more information from the groups than an outside moderator could.

Time Savings. Another reason some organizations prefer to do their own qualitative research is that they do not want to take the time to brief a moderator on the topic, or conform to the moderator's availability. They feel that they have much more time flexibility using internal corporate personnel who do not have outside scheduling conflicts.

Confidentiality. Occasionally an organization chooses to do its own qualitative research because it is dealing with a very confidential topic and fears that using an outside marketing professional might cause an information leak.

The Case for Using an Outsider

Expertise in Methodology. Research consultants generally do not have the same degree of knowledge about the research topic that people from the client organization do. But a research consultant does have a special expertise in conducting research. If conducting focus groups and one-on-ones seems easy when one is observing from behind a one-way mirror, it is probably because of the advance preparation and technical expertise of the moderator conducting the sessions. In fact, most organizations understand that expertise in *research methodologies* is far more important than *technical expertise* in the research topic, for obtaining a quality results from research.

Experience in Learning the Essentials. Experienced qualitative research consultants know how to gather enough information about a particular topic to be researched so that they can be effective facilitators in focus groups and one-on-ones. Further, when they encounter something they do not understand during the course of a session, they know to ask others in the group or the client personnel observing the session to explain it to them.

Moderator License. Most qualitative researchers feel that they are much more effective in focus groups and one-on-ones when the participants realize that they are *not* experts in the topic area but trained facilitators hired to stimulate discussion. This very important characteristic enables a moderator to ask questions that would be unacceptable from an "expert." Further, with a moderator who is not an expert in the area under discussion, the participants normally work harder to explain their views on the topic rather than try to impress the moderator with their knowledge of the topic using fancy language and terminology.

Objectivity. Perhaps the most prevalent argument in favor of using an outsider to conduct qualitative research is the *objectivity* this individual brings to the situation. Since the outside researcher has no "investment" in a group's outcome, most participants the researcher is much more objective during the session, and therefore will not try to lead them in any particular direction. Suppose a focus group is held to evaluate consumer reaction to a new advertising campaign idea. If this research is conducted by someone from the advertising agency, they could be perceived as leading the group to favor the concept the agency feels is best. Similarly, if the moderator is someone from the client organization, their ability or intention to objectively evaluate the discussion would be suspect. By using an outside researcher, the likelihood of getting an unbiased interpretation of the respondents is much greater.

Corporate Leverage. Many organizations believe that qualitative research results have much more impact with the ultimate decision makers if the research is conducted by an objective outsider. Some people in corporate organizations feel that focus groups that their own people implement are conducted to prove a point that supports their own view rather than to objectively seek consumer input on a topic of interest. Therefore, the involvement of the professional moderator can make the research results much more believable than they would be if internal people implemented the research.

Professionalism. An outside moderator will focus on the assignment and will not be distracted by the day-to-day "firefighting" that is common among people inside client organizations. As a result, the project will likely be completed on a faster timetable and in a more thorough manner than would be possible using in-house researchers.

Summary

Deciding whether to conduct research is often very difficult. If a company does not do research, it might miss some information that could be vital to the success of a program. But if it does conduct the research, it might spend significant money with little productive output. This chapter covered the most important issues that marketing professionals should address in deciding whether research should be conducted. The key factor is in the "cost/value" relationship of the research. If there is a good probability that the research will be productive, then it should be considered.

This chapter also examined issues that should be considered in determining whether qualitative or quantitative research should be employed, and whether a company should do its own qualitative research or hire an outsider. None of these are easy subjects, but with the information provided in this chapter, the reader will hopefully be better qualified to address them.

Research Decisions Outline

Should Research Be Implemented?
    Will the research cost exceed the value of the information?
    Is there enough time to do research?
    Can the research provide the information needed?
    Will the results of the research be believed and acted upon?
Should the Research be Qualitative or Quantitative?
    Budget

Timing
Projectability
Direct client involvement
Use of the research
Locale
Amount and type of information desired
Should the Research Be Done In-House or by an Outsider?
Advantages of in-house research
Cost savings
Expertise in company
Time savings
Confidentiality
Advantages of research by outsider
Expertise in methology
Experience in learning the essentials
Moderator license
Objectivity
Corporate leverage
Professionalism

3

Maximizing the Effectiveness of Focus Group Research

This chapter provides a series of suggestions on how moderators and clients can maximize the overall effectiveness of their focus group research. The basic premise behind this chapter is that an effective focus group program is a result of a disciplined process that comprises activities in the following three stages:

- *Before the Focus Groups.* Before the focus groups are conducted, the client should ensure that the right moderator has been selected, the correct participants are being recruited, and the proposed flow of discussion is consistent with the objectives of the study.
- *At the Focus Group Facility.* Immediately before and during the group coordination between client and moderator is needed to maximize the effectiveness of the research.
- *After the Focus Groups.* Some very important actions should be taken after each focus group and after the entire series of focus groups is completed. These will contribute to a more effective research program.

Activities before the Focus Groups

The planning process should begin as soon as it has been decided that focus groups are to be conducted. This process includes the following steps, each of which is vital to ensure that the client organization gets the most out the focus groups.

Establish the Research Objectives

The first step in an effective focus group project is to develop a brief (one-page) document that states the goals of the research, in terms of what the client wishes to learn from it. This presupposes "optimal" output from the groups and assumes that the participants are able to provide all the information that is desired.

Retain a Moderator

This vital step should be taken immediately after a commitment to do groups has been made and the research objectives established. Unfortunately, many organizations do not retain a moderator until much later in the process, because they do not appreciate the important role that the moderator can play as a consultant in focus group research as a whole, including planning. (How to select and evaluate moderators is the subject of Chapter 5.) Engaging a moderator early on is integral to effective focus group research.

Decide on the Executional Details of the Groups

The client and the moderator, working together, should determine the number of groups that will be conducted, the timing of the sessions, and their geographical location. The following guidelines should be helpful:

Number of Groups in the Series. The number of groups in a focus group series is often determined by the budget available for the research. While this is not the optimal way to develop a qualitative research program, it is the approach that is actually almost always employed to determine the number of groups in a series.

In the rare situation where budget is not the controlling issue, other factors should be considered. First, groups should almost always be conducted in multiples of two. Most moderators charge almost as much for one focus group as for two. This is because groups are normally conducted in the evening at six and eight o'clock, with each session lasting one and a half to one and three-quarters hours. Once a moderator has committed the evening for the research, the incremental time involved in conducting a second group is relatively small.

The moderator's preparation time is the same whether he or she is conducting one group or several. This includes such activities as writing the recruitment screening questions, developing the moderator guide, determining the "external stimuli" to be used during the session and finally writing the final report and maybe even providing a formal presentation to the client organization. All these activities take considerable time which normally is not a function of the number of focus groups in a series. Therefore, many moderators will charge only a little more to run a second group in an evening, since the only incremental time involved for the moderator is the extra two hours at the facility and the time it takes to listen to the tapes when developing the report.

Moreover, most field research services do not normally charge significantly more for use of the facility for one group than for two, since they cannot use the focus group room for another client that evening. Therefore, some of the "cost" of a second group is often built into that of the first group, making the second much more profitable.

The participants recruited for the groups should be as homogenous as possible in terms of their ages and sex. As discussed in detail in *The Practical Handbook and Guide to Focus Group Research,* men and women should ideally be in separate groups, and the age discrepancy of participants in the same group should not be more than fifteen years. Further, the criteria by which the participants are selected (like use of a product or service or a common attitude) should be applied consistently to facilitate the discussion and to help in the analysis of the output. Still, the reality of research budgets normally dictate compromises in these participant parameters, such as focus groups with business executives, physicians or other professionals when it can be difficult to find people who qualify for the session and the nature of the subject material is not such that men and women would have difficulty discussing it together.

Geographic Location of the Groups. This important factor can significantly influence the number of groups in a series. Deciding on the geographic location of the groups should be based on the following three key factors:

- *Location of the market.* The groups should be conducted in a specific market area. If a client is seeking to learn about attitudes toward a local newspaper, magazine, or retail store, it is necessary to hold the groups in that market. Climate can be a factor: research on snow blowers would have to be conducted in colder climates, whereas air-conditioner research would be more effective in warmer areas. Other factors that would require groups to be held in a specific market could be related to the volume of product usage (such as heavy use versus light), the incidence of various ethnic groups in the area, or existing distribution of the product.
- *Attitudes.* An attitude toward the product of service that differs according to geography is often a very important criterion in determining where groups are held. Many clients want to represent different market segments in a qualitative research study. A product or source may have a stronger franchise in some areas than in others, for example, or it may have received heavier advertising in some places than in others.
- *Competitive products.* Some client organizations may need to obtain inputs from consumers who shop in areas where specific competitive products are also available. This factor is often very important in determining the location of groups as when the client organization wants to learn how consumers feel about their product in relation to Competitor A in one area, while in another market it wants to see how consumers feel about it in relation to Competitor B.

Time of the Groups. Most focus groups are conducted at six and eight o'clock in the evening. But for some consumer segments it may be desirable to vary these times to facilitate recruitment of the participants. Target groups like physicians and business executives may prefer to attend at seven-thirty in the morning rather than in the evening. This should be considered in the planning process so it can be incorporated into the moderator's program for recruiting the participants.

There is definitely a trend today toward more use of daytime groups in order to accommodate the needs of the respondents, and the desires of many moderators and clients.

Brief the Moderator

In the briefing, the client provides the moderator with sufficient information to be able to:

- write an effective moderator guide that reflects the needs of the client and is consistent with the research objectives.
- be sufficiently informed about the research objectives so that he or she will be sensitive to the nuances that emerge during the group discussion.
- ask the right questions of the participants in order to obtain the information that the study is intended to provide.

In the briefing, it is essential that the client view the moderator as a partner in the research process rather than an outsider. A moderator's effectiveness during focus groups often depends heavily on the quality of the information provided during the briefing.

Develop a Screening Questionnaire

The moderator should develop a screening questionnaire that will be used to recruit participants based on specifications established by the client organization. This questionnaire is normally very brief (four to six questions) but it must be developed carefully to insure that the moderator recruits the correct people for the group.

A typical screening questionnaire is provided in figure 3–1.

Develop a Moderator Guide

The moderator guide is one of the three most important parts of the focus group process (along with the quality of the moderator and the correct recruiting of participants). It should be treated with the same degree of seriousness and attention to detail that is normally allocated to a quantitative research questionnaire.

A moderator guide is basically an outline of the discussion to be held during the focus group session. A well-written guide covers the following sections of the upcoming focus group:

- *Introduction.* Here the moderator will introduce him or herself to the participants, briefly explains the purpose of the session, and alerts them to the microphones or video cameras that are recording the sessions and the one-way

FIGURE 3–1

Typical Screening Questionnaire

Clarion - Skin Care Focus Group Screener

Name: _____   Home Phone: _____

Home Address: _____

City: _____   State: _____   Zip: _____

Hello, I'm from The Focus Center, an independent market research company in San Francisco. We're conducting a survey among people in the area about the skin care products they use and I would like to ask you a few questions.

Q1.   Do you or does anyone in your household work for any of the following industries: advertising, marketing research, or public relations, or a manufacturer of pharmaceuticals or skin care products?

Yes   *terminate and tally*

No   **continue**

Q2.   Have you participated in a group discussion, survey, or been asked to test any products for market research purposes in the past six months?

Yes   *terminate and tally*

No   **continue**

Q3.   Do you currently use over-the-counter sunscreen or sunblock?

Yes   **continue**

No   *terminate and tally*

Q4.   Do you have a skin type, problem, condition or treatment that affects your exposure to the sun or your choice of sunscreen?

Yes   **continue**

No   *terminate and tally*

Skin Care Focus Group Screener - Page Two

Q5.   Next I am going to read you a list of statements about skin care. Please tell me if any of the following statements apply to yourself. (Circle numbers for each statement).

     1   I use Retin A for skin problems such as wrinkles or acne

     2   I have had collagen implants

     3   I am allergic to normal sunscreen and must use a special non-allergenic formula

     4   I have had a skin cancer

     5   I have a medically diagnosed sensitivity to the sun and I require special protection from the sun

     6   I have had a chemical peel

     7   I have had a dermabrasion

     8   I take a drug such as Tetracycline that limits my exposure to the sun

     9   None of these apply to me   *terminate*

Q6.   Do you currently use a therapeutic skin care product such as Lubriderm or Keri?

Yes	*continue*
No	*terminate and tally*

Q7.   Which brand is that?

Keri	*continue*
Lubriderm	*continue*
Moisturelle	*continue*
Softeen	*Go to Q9.*
Complex 15	*continue*
Curel	*continue*
Other	*terminate and tally*

Q8.   Have you ever used or heard of a product called Softeen?

Yes	*continue*
No	*terminate and tally*

Q9.   Are you currently under the care of a dermatologist?

Yes	*continue*
No	*terminate and tally*

FIGURE 3–1

Typical Screening Questionnaire (continued)

Skin Care Focus Group Screener - Page Three

Q10.　Approximately how many times per year do you visit your dermatologist?
(DO NOT READ)
Less than 3　　　　　　　　　*terminate*
4 or more　　　　　　　　　**continue**

Q11.　Do you use bath oils or therapeutic bath products?
Yes　　　　　　　　　**continue**
No　　　　　　　　　**continue**

Q12.　Which of the following groups include your age?　(READ LIST)
Under 24　　　　　　　　　*terminate*
25 - 29　　　　　　　　　***Group 1 - 6:00***
30 - 39　　　　　　　　　***Group 1 - 6:00***
40 - 49　　　　　　　　　***Group 2 - 8:00***
50 - 59　　　　　　　　　***Group 2 - 8:00***
60 and Older　　　　　　　　　*terminate*

Q13.　Sex (by observation)
Male　　　　　　　　　***Check Quotas***
Female　　　　　　　　　***Check Quotas***

We would like you to come to our facility in San Francisco for a group discussion regarding your experience with sunblock and moisturizing products. This discussion will be held at The Focus Center on August 13, 1990 at 6:00 / 8:00 p.m. and will last approximately two hours. We are not trying to sell you anything. We only are interested in your opinions. For your participation, we will give you $50 in cash (6:00 - and dinner will be provided). Would you be willing to participate? (If yes, record information on first page of screener. If no, thank and terminate).

Before this discussion group on August 13, we would require you to use a new sunblock developed by a major pharmaceutical company. This new sunblock is non-allergenic and contains a sun protection factor (SPF) of 15. We will mail you samples of the product in a few days and ask that you use it 3 times prior to the discussion group.

mirror through which observers watch the session. Finally, the participants introduce themselves.

- *A warm-up.* Here the participants are asked to discuss very general issues related to the topic. For example, if a group is being held to expose people to a new concept in dog food, the warm-up would be used to learn basic information about the participants' dogs and how they feed them, including how often and the types of dog food they purchase. The moderator guide identifies all the topics that are to be covered in this warm-up discussion.

- *A details section.* Here discussion is intended to identify important information about the product category. In the dog food example, the moderator might have the participants discuss the advantages and disadvantages of the dog goods they currently buy, and what a manufacturer could do to make the optimal dog food. The moderator guide identifies in outline all the points the moderator should cover in this section of the group.

- *A key content section.* In this part of the group, input will be gained from the participants about the research topic itself. In the dog food example, the participants are exposed to several different concepts for new types of dog food. The guide identifies the areas that the moderator probes during this section in order to ensure that the discussion of the topic is thorough.

- *Summary.* The summary section gives the participants an opportunity to share any information about the topic that they may have forgotten or otherwise omitted. A common way to elicit this information is for the moderator to ask them to give "advice to the president" about the topic.

Unfortunately, in too many situations, a moderator enters a focus group facility with a one-page list of issues to address with the participants rather than a formal guide. The content of the typical moderator guide is discussed in great detail in *The Practical Handbook and Guide to Focus Group Research* and will not be repeated here. But a good moderator guide is vital to an effective focus group project.

Developing an effective moderator guide involves two principal steps. Depending on the complexity of the material and the skill of the moderator, however, these can be significantly extended. In the first step, the moderator develops an initial draft of the guide based on his or her understanding of the needs of the client as stated in the briefing. This draft should be as thorough as possible, covering all topics to be discussed during the focus group session. The draft should outline the information that the moderator plans to cover and list the specific external stimuli that will be used during the group to elicit information for the participants. (An external stimulus may be a product sample, a concept statement, an ad, or the like.) These must be identified in the guide to ensure that the client organization has a complete understanding of the material that will be presented during the group sessions.

Once the moderator has developed a draft of the guide, the client should review its content and suggest changes that would make it more consistent with the objectives of the research. The final version of the guide must be developed as a result of this interactive process between client and moderator to ensure that it reflects the needs of the client and is consistent with the procedural needs of the moderator.

The importance of the moderator guide cannot be underestimated, as it is very difficult for a moderator to achieve the client's research objectives if the guide has not been jointly developed by them and agreed upon well in advance of the sessions.

Select a Facility

There are thousands of different focus group facilities in the United States and most major cities offer several different choices. The focus group facility that is selected should meet the research needs in the following areas.

Physical Plant. The facility's physical plant should be conducive to quality focus groups—both the focus group room and the observation room behind the one-way mirror. When evaluating a facility's physical plant, these factors should be considered:

- Is the focus group room sufficiently large that the participants will not feel cramped during the session? A room that is too small can negatively affect the participants' ability to provide the maximum useful information. The room also should be large enough that the moderator can move around it easily, as it is often desirable to use an easel at the front of the room to record the participants' comments.

- Is the focus group room adequately soundproofed, both from street noise and from noises from other rooms or the outer areas of the facility? Few things are more annoying to clients, moderators, and participants than continuous distractions from outside noise during the course of a discussion.

- Is the observation room behind the one-way mirror comfortable for the people watching the sessions, in terms of its size and its physical amenities (a good viewing area, comfortable chairs, and the like)?

Recruitment Sources. In selecting a facility, the following should also be considered:

- Can the facility effectively recruit the correct participants based on the screening criteria established by the moderator and the client? Most moderators feel that the weakest link in the focus group research process is recruitment. The facility should be able to deliver the correct number of participants and ensure that they all meet the screening criteria. It must guarantee the moderator that it will deliver full groups of qualified people, recognizing that this will require it to over recruit by two to four people to make up for the inevitable "no-shows."

The most effective facilities have these resources for participant recruitment:

- In-house recruiting supervised by the management of the facility, to ensure the quality of the participants.
- A large in-house database of "fresh" respondents who can be recruited very quickly to meet the criteria for the research.
- The ability to recruit effectively, using client lists, if this is desired.

- Experience in recruiting the types of people needed. If the specifications call for recruiting of dermatologists, for example, the facility must have prior experience in recruiting among dermatologists, or the results could be disappointing.

Costs. Cost competiveness should also be considered, in light of the services that the client organization requests. This does not mean that the lowest-cost facility should be selected. Rather, the facility should charge a fair cost for the services it provides. (The costs of focus group research are discussed in great detail in Chapter 6.)

Develop a Rescreening Questionnaire

It is always advisable for the moderator to direct the focus group facility to rescreen all the participants in the group *before* they are accepted as qualified. This process, which normally takes less than two minutes, ensures that the people who participate in the discussion meet all the screening criteria that have been established. It simply involves asking the people as they arrive at the facility a few brief questions to ensure that they meet the criteria, since telephone recruiters occasionally accept people who do not meet all the criteria.

A rescreening questionnaire should be developed at the same time as the screening questionnaire. It simply uses questions from the original screening questionnaire. The facility should be told that it will be expected to rescreen all participants and that it will be given a rescreening questionnaire. It is important that the rescreener be made up of questions that were asked in the original recruitment questionnaire, to ensure consistency between the two.

The rescreening questionnaire might include an "articulation" question in order to ensure that a participant can think well enough to be an effecive participant. An articulation question is a subjective, open-ended query about a topic of general interest, that forces prospective participants to demonstrate their ability to communicate reasonably well. Examples of articulation questions are: "Please tell me what you think about the coup in the Soviet Union," or "Do you feel that the national debt is a real problem, or is it used as a political tool by the party out of power?" "How do you feel about federal government subsidies to private schools?" When an articulation question is used, it is generally not necessary to record the answers. Rather, the purpose is to minimize the probability that the participant will be unable to communicate effectively during the session.

Activities at the Focus Group Facility

A few important activities should occur at the focus group facility, when the client and moderator arrive for the groups. These will improve the effectiveness of the sessions.

Supervise the Rescreening of Participants

In the earlier planning stage, the rescreening questionnaire was discussed, as was the need to direct the facility to rescreen. The client or the moderator must supervise the the facility people on duty at the time of the groups so that they understand what is expected of them in the rescreening process. The rescreening must be done away from the main reception area so that the people who are in line or waiting to sign in do not hear the answers provided by those who precede them. The moderator should arrange for the clients in the observation room to be given the original screening questionnaires (and also the rescreeners when they are completed) when they arrive, so that they can review the composition of the group before the session. This is important as it may be necessary to send one or two people home if all the prospects show up for the group, and often the information in the screeners will identify the people who are the least qualified for participation.

Provide Food for the Participants

In more than half of all focus group sessions, the participants are provided with a meal while in the remainder they are given a light snack (like cookies and soft drinks). A key issue between the moderator and the facility is to coordinate when to feed the participants, to decide whether they will be permitted to eat during the session, and to arrange how the food and dishes will be cleaned up if the people do eat during the session.

My feelings about this issue are that it is generally better to feed the participants *before* they enter the focus group room, as this significantly reduces the clutter on the table. It is often difficult to see a participant's nametag if there are beverage glasses, soft drink cans, and the like on the table. Further, if the participants are asked to do any writing during the session, the plates, soda cans, and cups can get in the way and be a significant disturbance. Finally, if the discussion involves the use of external stimuli (like concept boards and product prototypes), they may become soiled by the "garbage" on the table from the meal.

In many situations, however, there is not sufficient time for the participants to eat before they enter the focus group room, and so food is brought into the session itself. In these situations, the moderator should encourage the participants to discard their waste and plates in a receptacle in the room as soon as they have finished eating. It is *not* desirable to have someone from the facility enter the room during the session to clean up, as this is very disruptive and can affect the participants' concentration on the topic.

Manage the Noise Level

When the moderator arrives at the facility, he or she should emphasize to the management that it must be very quiet outside the room during the session. Unless this point is made very strongly, it is likely that there will be problems with noise from the facility staff as they talk among themselves or on the telephone. Another common source of noise is early arrivals signing in for the next group around the main desk, or the end of a group session in another room.

Provide Nametags for the Participants

It is very important that each participant have a nametag that is visible from the observation room so that the client observers can see all the participants' names. For nametags, I suggest:

- Use only first names, even if the participants have titles (like doctor or general). This makes the environment much less formal and keeps titles from getting in the way of the process.
- Ensure that the name on the tag is the one by which the participant likes to be called, not necessarily the name on

the screening questionnaire by which the person was recruited. Many facilities like to prepare nametags before the participants arrive, using the screening questionnaires. But people named Joseph often want to be called Joe, for example, or an Elizabeth may want to be called Muffy. People respond much better when addressed by their most commonly used name, and this is what should be put on the tag.

- Ensure that the name is written on both sides of the tag, so that the moderator can see the name from all over the room. Many facilities write only on the front, yet when the moderator gets to the back of the room to write on the board, it becomes impossible to see the participants' names.

Tell the Facility How Many Participants to Admit and What to Do with Late Arrivals

Virtually all facilities overrecruit for focus groups to compensate for "no-shows," who are generally about 20 percent of the people who agree to participate in a session. The moderator must coordinate with the facility so that both parties know what to do if everyone who was recruited shows up and how to handle late arrivals. The moderator should:

Decide on the Optimal Number of Participants for the Session. The most common approach is to use ten people for a full group and five or six for a minigroup. If the number of people who arrive exceeds the desired maximum, most moderators will advise the facility to send the "excess" home (after paying them for their time) rather than have too many people in the group.

Select the Most Desirable People to Participate. This is often difficult to do, as you don't want to turn away a participant who could make a major contribution to the session in favor of one who does not. To help ensure that the most qualified people participate in the session, I suggest the following process:

1. Choose the people who *best* meet the recruitment criteria. Those who do so marginally should be eliminated first.

2. Try to configure the most age-homogeneous group by eliminating the people who are well above or below the average age of the group. The more homogeneous the group, the better the participants will relate to each other in the discussion.
3. Eliminate people who appear unlikely to contribute meaningfully to the discussion. This is a subjective judgment that should be made jointly between the moderator and the facility staff. They should consider such factors as:
   - attitude problems toward the group or the topic
   - excessive shyness
   - language problems
   - hearing problems
   - extremely poor eyesight
   - answers to the articulation question

Have the Facility Turn the Excess people Away Without Alienating Them. Most facilities have their own way of explaining that they overbook due to "no-shows" and that people turned away will be paid for their time. In virtually all cases, this is sufficient, and non-participants are happy to leave with their payment. But this discussion should occur *after* the participants have entered the focus group room.

Instruct the Facility to Handle Late Arrivals. In many cases, it is necessary to begin a focus group session before the full complement of participants have arrived at the facility, or too much time will be lost. This is a particular problem with evening groups: if a six o'clock session does not start until 6:20, valuable time is lost *or* the next session, at eight, will start late. It is essential for the moderator to instruct the facility what to do with latecomers when they arrive.

- Some moderators are comfortable with the latecomers entering the room whenever they arrive, in order to have enough people for a full group.
- Other moderators feel that once the door has been closed, new people entering the room are too disruptive, and they do not permit latecomers in the session.

The moderator's preference regarding latecomers must be conveyed to the facility to ensure that the session does not get distracted. Most moderators do not authorize the facility to pay late-comers who arrive more than ten minutes after the start of the session.

Ensure That the Room Is Set Up Properly

Small details of the focus group process are very important to the overall quality of the session. Consider these factors:

Visibility. The group room should be set up so that the clients in the observation room will be able to see all the participants' faces. While most facilities are cognizant of this fact and configure their rooms properly, occasionally a facility will seat participants so that their backs or profiles face the mirror, and the clients have difficulty following what they are saying.

Easel Placement. The easel should be placed in a position in the room that is most advantageous to the needs of the client organization. I prefer the easel to be at the opposite end of the room from the client observers so they can see what is being written on it. Others prefer that the easel face the participants, which obscures what is written on it from the people in the observation room. The key factor to consider here is the relative importance of seeing the participants' faces while the moderator is collecting information and opinions from them at the easel. If it is important to see the faces then the easel should be obscured, but if what is written is key, the faces should be obscured.

Writing Supplies. Each participant should have a pad and pencil in front of them, in the event that the moderator asks them to write down their reactions to ideas during the group.

Temperature. The temperature of the room should be neither too hot nor too cold. Either of these would adversely affect the participation of the group.

Conduct a Moderator's Briefing before the Session

The moderator's briefing informs the client observers what will be happening during the session, including:

- *the objectives of the session,* including what is desired from it and what the moderator feels can and cannot be learned from it.
- *the intended flow of the discussion.* The moderator reviews the content of the moderator guide with the observers, and they make any last-minute changes in it that are deemed necessary.
- *the external stimuli that will be used during the group to elicit responses from the participants,* such as concepts, product prototypes, and the like.
- *tips on proper viewing techniques* that can help the observers can get more information out of the group. Observers can be advised to look for nonverbal participant reactions and to watch for the "big idea" rather than focus on the comments of one outspoken participant.

Coordinate Communication between the Moderator and the Client Observers

Specifically, the client and the moderator should discuss how they will communicate with each other during the session, to ensure that the observers have input into the direction of the discussion.

Note-Passing. The process of communication between the moderator and the client observers has changed in recent years. In the early days of focus group research, client observers communicated with the moderator by sending a note into the room when they wanted a question asked of the group, or wanted another area explored as a result of comments from the participants. But today most experienced moderators do not advise using notes from the observation room as a means of communication for several reasons.

One reason is that when a note is brought into the room, it disrupts the flow of conversation as the participants watch the person deliver the note to the moderator. This phenomenon can significantly impact on the flow of discussion and waste valuable time while the moderator gets the discussion back on track.

Another reason is that upon receipt of the note, the moderator has to read it, interpret what it means (often deciphering difficult-to-read handwriting), then figure out where and how to introduce the note material into the group. This takes the moderator's attention away from directing the group and can result in some very unproductive time during the session.

Still another reason notes are no longer preferred is that the ease of sending notes from the observation room to the moderator allows some clients to get into a habit of constantly sending notes, thus affecting the moderator's ability to follow the discussion flow as set out in the guide. This can make it difficult to cover all the topics in the guide, since the moderator is forced to constantly change direction by introducing the additional topics from the observation room.

Finally, perhaps the most important reason to prohibit the use of notes relates to the role of the moderator in the process as a whole. One of the main reasons that focus groups work as a research technique is that the moderator is the *authority figure* in the room. This status allows the moderator to request the participants to follow the prescribed "program," to conduct the flow of the discussion, and to undertake other activities. I have found that when notes are passed into the room from the clients, the moderator loses the position of authority since it becomes obvious to the participants that the people in the back are really in control. Often the participants begin to talk to the mirror rather than to the moderator, since they feel the more important people are behind the mirror. This makes it difficult for the moderator to effectively control the focus group.

Leaving the Room. How then should clients communicate with the moderator? This is where effective advance planning becomes particularly important. When the moderator develops the guide, observation room interaction should be planned and built into the flow of the discussion. The moderator should be given a way to leave the room and go to the observation room for brief discussions.

Doing this without negatively affecting group dynamics requires significant planning and agreement by both parties. The moderator needs to plan the visits in such a way that they do not affect the flow of discussion. Specifically, the participants should not talk to each other while the moderator is out of the room, since there is no control over what is said and one member of the group may create a major bias in the others during the moderator's absence. As a result, the moderator should organize the activities in the focus group room so that the participants have something to do (read, write, or draw) while the moderator is away that will preclude discussion among them. They may be asked to write down their feelings about a particular concept, or how they use a specific product, or what the criteria for the "ideal" product would be. Other possibilities are to ask them to read a long concept statement or draw a picture that indicates their feelings about a particular topic. As we will see in Chapter 7, the moderator can use this time to great advantage if the group has productive things to do.

The clients, for their part, should understand before the group begins that the moderator will come to the observation room several times during the session to communicate with them. This "planned visitation" should eliminate the knee-jerk need of some clients to send a note every time they get an idea. They know it will be possible to talk directly with the moderator about their idea in a few minutes during the visit. The client observers must prioritize their comments with the moderator, as it is not advisable to spend more than thirty to forty-five seconds at a time away from the focus group room, or it can affect the dynamics of the group. Therefore, only essential issues should be discussed.

With a planned program of face-to-face communication with the moderator, the client observers become a meaningful part of the focus group process, and the moderator can integrate the material they suggest into the discussion in a way that does not disrupt the flow of the session.

Conduct a Postgroup Discussion

Before the groups begin, the client observers and the moderator should agree to remain at the facility for fifteen to twenty minutes after the last group for a short debriefing. This important part of the focus group process enables everyone involved to express their overall feelings about the sessions while the experience is still fresh in their minds. It also enables the moderator to note any serious disagreements among the client personnel or between himself and the client, which need to be handled in subsequent focus groups or in the moderator's report.

Finally, the postsession discussion gives the moderator an opportunity to share with the client some overall observations about the content that the group generated or about changes that should be proposed for future groups. One major advantage of focus group research is the evolutionary nature of the process; the postgroup discussion often serves as a catalyst for changing the guide or the presentation of concepts, applying what has been learned from one session to the next.

Planning the postgroup discussion involves telling people that it will be held. Knowing about the discussion in advance encourages the observers to take notes and prepare mentally for the discussion that will follow. This results in a more productive interchange in the discussion.

Activities after the Focus Groups

The postgroup period is the time between the completion of the groups and the client organization's approval of the final report. Planning in advance the elements in this stage avoids either party becoming upset with the other due to unfulfilled expectations.

The factors that need to be considered in this postgroup period are:

- When does the client expect to receive the final report?
- What form should the final report have? As covered in detail in *The Practical Handbook and Guide to Focus Group Research,* there are several different approaches to writing final reports. It is essential that both parties agree on what will be delivered.
- Will the final presentation be delivered personally, in the form of a stand-up presentation, or will a written report be mailed to the client?
- What expectations, if any, does the client have of the moderator after the final report has been delivered? Is the moderator expected to be available for follow-up meetings to plan future stages of process? Is the moderator expected to revise the report if it needs to be condensed for other persons within the client organization?

Summary

The focus group process will work better if the client and the moderator follow a series of relatively simple and predictable steps in planning the sessions. This chapter reviewed the planning steps that need to be done for three major phases of the focus group process (before the groups, at the facility, after the groups). Following this process will greatly increase the probability that the results of the process will meet both the client's and the moderator's expectations.

Effectiveness Outline

Activities before the Focus Groups
    Establish the research objectives
    Retain a moderator
    Decide on the executional details
        Number of groups
        Geographic location of the groups
        Time of the groups
    Brief the moderator
    Develop the screening questionnaire
    Develop the moderator guide
    Select a facility, based on its:
        Physical plant
        Recruitment services
        Costs
    Develop a rescreening questionnaire
Activities at the Focus Group Facility
    Supervise the rescreening of participants
    Provide food for the participants
    Manage the noise level
    Provide nametags for the participants
    Instruct the facility on extra participants and late arrivals
    Ensure that the room is properly set up
        Visibility
        Easel placement
        Writing supplies
        Temperature
    Conduct a moderator's briefing
    Coordinate communication between moderator and client observers
    Conduct a postgroup discussion
Activities after the Focus Groups: The Final Report

4

Common Mistakes in Focus Groups

The many fans of focus groups believe them to be an extremely valuable market research technique that can meaningfully contribute to a research effort. At the same time, there are many marketing professionals who discourage the use of focus groups, either because of a concern with the basic methodology (the pressure of group interviews with a limited number of people) or because they have had bad experiences with it.

It is my strong feeling that most of the bad experiences that organizations have had with focus groups could have been avoided if sufficient time had been allocated to the planning process *and* if the clients were more aware of the mistakes commonly made in focus group projects.

This chapter identifies the most common errors that organizations make in the use of focus groups, and where appropriate, it suggests alternatives to consider and ways to avoid making the mistakes in the future. Mistakes made in the focus group process essentially fall into three major categories.

- *Methodological Mistakes.* These involve attempting to use focus groups to accomplish objectives that are not realistic in the light of their capabilities.
- *Procedural Mistakes.* These include errors made in implementation and in the involvement of key people in the various stages of the process.
- *Analytical Mistakes.* These errors result from inappropriate interpretation of the output of focus groups.

Methodological Mistakes

The most common methodological mistakes in focus group research are as follows.

Using Focus Groups Where Quantitative Research Is Needed

It is quite common for organizations to decide to conduct focus groups because insufficient time or funding is available to implement a quantitative study. But focus groups should not be considered as an alternative to a quantitative study, since the objectives and capabilities of each technique are quite different. The output of a focus group study is not likely to be valuable if a different research methodology is more appropriate for the given situation.

To minimize the chances of facing this type of methodological dilemma, it is strongly recommended that a *written* statement of the specific research objectives be developed well before the actual study is to be implemented. This statement of objectives should identify specifically what the client wants to learn from the research. By analyzing the research objectives, a research professional can easily identify the type of methodology that is appropriate and that stays within the budgetary and timing parameters. The researcher should advise the client about limitations of various possible methodologies in light of the research objectives. If meeting the research objectives requires the use of a methodology that the client does not want to use (such as a quantitative technique), it is advisable that the client modify the research objectives. This is very important because if the objectives are not modified, it will be virtually impossible for the client to be satisfied with the output of the research, since the methodology will not be able to produce the information that the client needs.

Using Focus Groups as a Decision-Making "Tiebreaker"

Some client organizations feel that virtually every decision they make must be based on "research," and they like to use focus groups as a quick and easy aid in this process. Therefore, each time they need to make a meaningful decision, they order a focus group. The output from the group becomes the deciding factor in making the decision.

This is not the correct way to use focus group research. As discussed in Chapter 1, focus groups are a *qualitative* methodology and are not intended to provide definitive answers to questions. They can be very helpful in providing inputs into a decision-making process and in helping design a research instrument that can provide statistically reliable data. But it is generally not advisable to use focus groups to make decisions. There are other research approaches that can accomplish this with greater accuracy and reliability.

Using Focus Groups to Generate New Product Ideas

Some client organizations feel that the concept for their next "million-dollar" product will emerge from a focus group session, and they use the technique to try to elicit this type of information. Such clients see focus groups as a type of brainstorming session to generate new product ideas. Some organizations even ask the participants what new products they would like see developed. While focus groups play a very important role in new product development, they are rarely a source of new product ideas. If a client's expectation of a focus group is to come out with the concept for their next new product, the chances are very great that they will be extremely disappointed.

The reasons for this are several.

- In the first place, the typical participant does not think in terms of new product ideas. Almost everyone occasionally comes up with an idea that they feel would make a very successful new product, but when asked for such input "on demand," most people are not very productive. Participants in focus groups can be very helpful in *reacting* to new product ideas that are presented to them during a session, but they almost never are the source of a new product idea themselves.
- Nor is the focus group technique itself designed to create

new product ideas. Brainstorming and Synectics are much better techniques for developing the strengths of a group to achieve this objective.

When new product ideas are generated from focus group research, they tend to come from the client organization's interpretation of the inputs of the participants rather than from the specific ideas the participants provided. The idea for the campaign to advertise baking soda as an "odor eater" for refrigerators, for example, came out of a focus group exploring the different ways people use baking soda. During the course of the discussion, one of the participants said they put a box of baking soda in their refrigerator to remove the odors. This idea was picked up by an assistant product manager at Church & Dwight (the Arm & Hammer Company) who ultimately convinced management and its advertising agency to market this benefit as a key use for Arm & Hammer baking soda.

Using Focus Groups to Predict the Sales of a Product or Service

While focus groups can be extremely helpful in learning consumer reactions to a product, they are not effective in predicting the future sales volume. That task requires a quantitative methodology that will employ a larger, projectable sample and a questionnaire designed to address this type of issue.

Using Focus Groups to Determine Awareness of an Advertising Campaign

Focus groups can be a very effective *part* of a program to assess the effectiveness of an advertising campaign. But the technique is not appropriate for determining absolute levels of awareness. Gaining this type of information requires quantitative methods that employ large, projectable samples. The role of focus groups here should be to ascertain consumer attitudes toward the campaign, to help determine how well the campaign communicates the intended message, and to identify parts of the message that are not believable or easily understood. When this qualitative input is combined with quantitative results, it should provide a significant amount of meaningful information about the campaign.

Using Focus Groups to Sell Products

The most serious violation of focus group research is to use the groups ostensibly for research purposes but in reality to capture the attention of a target group for up to two hours to sell products. In the medical community, for example, some drug and drug-related companies recruit physicians for "focus group research," when their real objective is to convince the physicians to prescribe their products rather than those of the competition. This abuse of the technique gives focus groups a bad name and makes it more difficult (and expensive) to gain the participation of difficult-to-reach target customers for legitimate research.

Procedural Mistakes

Some mistakes are commonly made in the *implementation* of focus groups. The procedural mistakes discussed in this section can all be avoided if the user of the research is aware of them *and* is willing to make the extra effort to correct them.

These are the most common procedural mistakes that are made in focus groups.

The Research Objectives Are Not Clearly Defined

Much time can be wasted in planning research when those involved in the project lack a clear understanding of what the objectives of the study are. In the worst-case scenario, this error results in focus groups that are useless, since they were conceived with the wrong objectives. In less destructive situations, this error simply wastes the client's and the moderator's time in preparing for the group before the "correct" research objective is established.

The Participants Are Unsuitable

As in most market research techniques, the quality of focus group output is extremely dependent on the quality of the participants. If the right people are not recruited for a focus group, the information that the session generates may be unhelpful or even worthless. Properly defining the participants may seem basic, but failure to do so is one of the most common mistakes in configuring focus groups. Problems usually occur because neither the client nor the moderator has carefully thought out the characteristics of the participants who would provide the most valuable input into the sessions. Typical errors in recruitment include:

Participants Are Insufficiently Aware of the Product. People who are insufficiently aware of the product or service to be discussed will not provide meaningful, substantive input. I recall a focus group conducted for a bank in a major metropolitan area to gain inputs on the feelings of older citizens toward the various special service programs that banks offer them. The mistake was that the recruiting questionnaire did not ask about the potential participants' awareness of the bank or of the service programs banks offer. Ten minutes into the focus group, it became clear that none of the participants were familiar with the bank or had even heard of the special service programs.

Participants Have Only Positive Feelings About the Product. Many focus groups are intended to learn what is *wrong* about a product or service in order to make the appropriate changes to improve it. Unfortunately, such focus groups are commonly composed of the regular or heavy users of the product or service, under the assumption that they are most knowledgeable about it and therefore can provide the best quality input. The mistake here is that the regular users of a product or service are normally quite satisfied with it and have relatively minor dissatisfactions. Groups configured with "tryer rejectors," a people who once used the product or service but no longer do, often produce significantly more useful output. Because these people were dissatisfied enough to reject the product or service, hearing their reasons can be very important to fixing the problems.

The Participants Are Not Sufficiently Homogeneous

As discussed in detail in *The Practical Handbook and Guide to Focus Group Research,* the more homogeneous the group is, the better the participants will relate to each other and the higher the quality of the input they will generate. These rules of thumb are very helpful in configuring focus groups:

- Men and women should be in separate groups whenever possible. This is particularly important when conducting research among persons less than thirty years old.
- The youngest participant in the room should not be more than fifteen years younger than the oldest participant.
- People from very different socioeconomic groups or with very different educational levels should be in separate groups, if possible, even if they all are users of the product or service.
- Children's groups should not include anyone below the third grade. No more than a two-grade spread should be used with children between the ages of eight and fifteen.

The Moderator Is Inadequate

It is generally recognized throughout the research industry that the most important element in the focus group process is the moderator. The right moderator can make the difference between successful groups that provide excellent information for the client, and ones that provide misleading information that ultimately costs the client both time and money. (Chapter 5 discusses the role of the moderator in the focus group process and the characteristics of the ideal moderator. It also suggests ways that clients can evaluate moderators).

The Facility Cannot Recruit the Right Participants

There are major differences among focus group facilities in their ability to recruit participants. Some employ a staff of highly trained in-house interviewers who are tightly supervised in order to maintain quality control. Others "farm out" the recruiting to independent contractors who do the telephoning from their homes.

Quality recruiting is vital for effective focus groups, as the wrong participants will not contribute to meeting the research objectives of the groups. Quality recruiting organizations are willing to *guarantee* that they can deliver the right number of participants for each session and that all of them will meet the screening specifications.

The Facility's Physical Plant Is Deficient

The overall quality of the physical plant can significantly affect the results of the research. Problems may include:

The Observation Room Is Inadequate. This could be because the room is uncomfortable, too small, or not sufficiently ventilated, or it does not have enough "window" space to permit everyone to observe the proceedings through the mirror. A bad viewing room can significantly affect the overall attitude of the observers and their ability to focus on the group discussion.

The Focus Group Room Is Too Small. Some older facilities in the United States have very small group rooms that require the participants to sit too close together during the session. If the participants are not comfortable, they will be less effective. Further, small group rooms do not enable the moderator to move around the room to use an easel or blackboard, or simply to change positions to energize the group.

The Facility Is Not Sufficiently Soundproofed. Focus group rooms that pick up sounds from outside (like street noises) or from other activities going on in the facility create major problems for a session. The noises can be very disruptive to the group, as it reduces the participants' ability to concentrate on the discussion.

The Facility Staff Is Badly Trained or Insensitive. It is *very* important that both the participants and the client personnel be made to feel very comfortable at the facility, so they are able to contribute at their maximum level.

The Moderator Guide Is Given Insufficient Attention

The moderator guide is one of the most important parts of the focus group process, along with the selection of the moderator and the participants. Sufficient time and attention must be given to the guide to ensure that it reflects the needs of the client and will produce a session that achieves the research objectives. I strongly recommend that the moderator guide be developed well in advance of the groups, so that the client personnel can study it and provide inputs to the moderator, assuring that the material covered by the guide is consistent with the research objectives.

While the importance of developing an effective guide may seem obvious, my experience suggests that some moderators and clients do not appreciate it. Some moderators show up for groups with no formal guide but only a few notes scribbled on paper. Others market themselves as effective "walk-on" moderators, in that they can arrive at a group session with virtually no advance preparation and still conduct an effective session.

As a general rule, the moderator and the client should give as much—or more—attention to developing the moderator guide as they would to preparing a questionnaire for a quantitative study.

The External Stimuli Are Inadequate

Focus groups are usually much more effective if the participants are exposed to specific materials to which they can react. This stimulates their thinking about the topic. Unfortunately, even when clients and moderators produce a good moderator guide, they often do not consider how to *implement* the guide. The result is frequently a last-minute scramble to develop a concept statement, to procure product samples, and the like. External stimuli that are commonly used in focus group research include:

- A product prototype, to show the participants what the final product will look like. Most prototypes are *not* working models of the product but are wooden, plastic, or cardboard representations of it as it is expected to look.
- A new product concept statement, in the form of a brief description of the idea. Sometimes a graphic representation is included.
- A packaging sample.
- A prototype (or actual) print or broadcast commercial.
- A rough art drawing of a promotional campaign.

All these types of external stimuli are frequently helpful in securing inputs from participants about an advertising or promotional concept, a new product being evaluated, or a series of packaging alternatives. The mistake that too many organizations make is that they spend insufficient time working on the concepts, prototypes, or rough ideas before the moderator presents them to the groups. As a result, the output from the sessions is not as useful as it might otherwise be. In preparing to research consumer reactions to several new product ideas, for example concept descriptions must be written very carefully, so that they communicate the ideas to the participants as clearly as possible. Further, it is important that each idea presented be meaningfully different from the others, or it will be very difficult to obtain an unbiased reaction to each.

In preparing external stimuli for focus group research, it is vital to follow these principles:

- They should be as simple as possible, to ensure that they are understood.
- They should be appropriate for the research objectives.
- The number of *different* stimuli should be kept to a maximum of four to six, as most participants have difficulty differentiating among more than that.

The Moderator Fails to Control the Group Dynamics

Sometimes the moderator does not know how to leverage group dynamics during a focus group session. The most serious problem that can arise is when a few individual participants are allowed to affect the participation of others. Unless special care is taken during the discussion, one or two dominant participants can significantly influence others' in reactions to specific ideas and reporting of personal behavior. This is perhaps the biggest concern of critics of the focus group technique, and it is one reason why some professionals prefer one-on-one interviews. If three participants say they never feed red meat to their families because of concerns over fat and cholesterol, for example, their comments can intimidate and inhibit the others, so that those who do buy red meat will say they don't, for fear of looking stupid or noncaring in front of their peers.

Interaction among participants is a vital part of the focus group process and must be encouraged in order to maximize the quality of the output from the session. If a session does not contain significant interaction among the people in the room, then the client loses one of the most important benefits of focus groups.

There are several techniques that a moderator can use to dramatically minimize or even eliminate the negative aspects of group dynamics and others that will maximize the positive benefits of the interaction (see Chapter 7). It is very important for the moderator to become familiar with them and build them into the guide to ensure that they are incorporated into the discussion.

Analytical Mistakes

Analytical mistakes are errors in the interpretation of focus group results on the part of researchers and client organizations. One of the greatest disadvantages of the focus group technique is its highly subjective nature: It permits observers to interpret to what happened during the group. One observer's interpretation may or may not be consistent with those of other observers. This section discusses the key areas where analytical errors are often made, so that clients and moderators can take appropriate action to minimize these problems.

The Observers Are Biased

The biggest analytical mistake people make is to enter the research with a preconceived bias and to listen for inputs from group participants that seem to confirm their belief. Unfortunately, this mistake is quite common in focus group research. Here are two examples of how a preexisting personal bias affected the interpretation of a group's output.

A radio station conducted focus groups to obtain listener inputs about a new program it was considering. In reality, the station manager was only interested in confirming his own belief in the viability of this new program so that he could tell senior management that research had been conducted and they would then permit him to air the program. The program being researched had been conceived by the station manager, so he had a considerable personal "investment" in the outcome of the research. The participants did not respond positively to the program, yet the manager chose to discount this input and air the program anyway. He rationalized that the groups had not been conducted very well, that the concept had not been effectively presented, and that the best respondents had not been recruited for the sessions. So it happened, the program lasted only a few months, as viewer reaction was so negative that it was quickly canceled.

An entrepreneur decided to utilize focus groups to get reactions to a new product he had invented that he thought would revolutionize the take-home fast-food market. He thought the product concept would offer significant benefits to consumers of fast food. The focus groups clearly indicated that the product offered no meaningful consumer appeal, that further concept exploration should be terminated, and that resources should be allocated to some other, more promising idea. But the entrepreneur was unable to accept these findings because of his emotional and financial commitment to the concept. He continued to invest in both research and product development to modify it. It took another six months and many thousands of dollars before he finally realized that the output from the groups had been valid.

It is very important for the moderator to maintain a completely objective perspective throughout the process so that the final report accurately reports the factual information from the groups and provides in independent interpretation.

The Results Are Quantified

Another common analytical mistake is trying to quantify the results of focus groups. It is not uncommon for analyses of groups to include discussions of why two people said one thing and three another, and to determine what percentage of the total respondents felt one way or another. In other situations, researchers attempt to project the attitudes of the group to the total universe, saying that since X number of participants were in favor of the idea, a certain portion of the total market would buy the product. But focus group methodology is not designed to provide projectable results to a larger universe, because the participants are not necessarily selected at random and because the sample size of the groups is small.

Too Much Emphasis Is Placed on the Inputs of a Few Participants

The people observing a group discussion often place too much importance on the comments made by a minority segment of the group because it agrees with their personal feelings about the topic.

This is not to suggest that minority inputs are not important or should not be used in the analysis. Rather, the analysis should focus on the "big picture" rather than on individual comments. The most effective way to evaluate focus groups is to try to identify the few really important findings of the group, considering the group's overall feelings about:

- the major strengths and weaknesses of the concept
- the key points the advertisement was communicating
- the overall image of the product being evaluated.

It is the responsibility of the moderator to base his or her conclusions on the overall "sense" of the participants about the topic under discussion and to use the atypical comments of individuals as potential areas of future exploration for the client organization.

The Final Report Is Misused

The final report is often the most important part of the research effort since it is the vehicle by which the moderator objectively interprets the group discussion. But sometimes focus group reports are not used properly:

Omitting the Report Altogether. Some clients do not require the moderator to write a final report following the groups, thinking that that way they will save some money. Instead, they have one of their own people summarize the groups, or they just hold an informal postgroup discussion to get the views of the various people in attendance. Neither approach is generally in the best interest of client organizations, for two primary reasons:

- The client does not receive the objectivity and perspective of an independent assessment. Moderators are normally much more objective than in-house people in interpreting focus group discussions.
- A final report gives the client organization a formal record of the proceedings to which it can refer in the future, when questions arise about the outputs of the group or when new people in the project need to be updated on the work done thus far.

Requiring the Report to Contain Verbatims. Some clients expect the report to contain verbatim quotations from the participants, to serve as capsule summaries of the tone of the discussion. Some also feel that quotations support the analysis made in the report. But is not only unnecessary but undesirable. It is unnecessary because interested parties can always refer to the audio or video record of the groups to get all the verbatims they need—in context. It is undesirable because it can significantly extend the time it takes to develop the report and normally increases the total cost of the research. Moreover, when moderators use verbatims in their reports, they may well select the statements that best support their analysis of the research, taking them out of context. Many very good moderators feel that verbatims are often used as "filler" in reports to make them seem more substantive, when the verbatims actually detract from the substance by shifting the focus of the report away from the "big picture."

Long reports with multiple verbatims also tend to be very difficult to read quickly to get the most important information. Senior management commonly chooses not to read a lengthy, quotation-filled report, and the project team loses the benefit of management's inputs to the research.

Summary

Knowing the errors commonly made by some companies in focus group research can be the most important factor in avoiding future errors. This chapter has discussed the most common such mistakes and suggested actions to take to eliminate them in your focus group studies.

Common Mistakes Outline

Methodological Mistakes
   Using focus groups where quantitative research is needed
   Using focus groups as decision-making "tiebreaker"
   Using focus groups to generate new ideas
   Using focus groups to predict sales
   Using focus groups to determine awareness of advertising campaign
   Using focus groups to sell products
Procedural Mistakes

The research objectives are not clearly defined
The participants are unsuitable
    Are insufficiently aware of the product
    Have only positive feelings about the product
The participants are not sufficiently homogeneous
The moderator is inadequate
The facility cannot recruit the right participants
The facility's physical plant is deficient
The guide is given insufficient attention
The external stimuli are inadequate
The moderator fails to control the group dynamics
Analytical Mistakes
    The observers are biased
    The results are quantified
    Too much emphasis is placed on the inputs of one or two participants
    The final report is misused
        Omitting the report altogether
        Requiring the report to contain verbatims

5

The Moderator

Few people involved in qualitative research today would not agree that the most important element in the focus group process is the moderator. The moderator is often compared to an orchestra leader, in that he or she sets the tone for the session and directs it in such a way that the research objectives are achieved. Further, an effective moderator will do a great deal of preparation in advance of the groups, as does an orchestra leader before conducting a symphony.

The objectives of this chapter are:

- to discuss the role of the moderator in the research process
- to describe the key characteristics of an effective moderator
- to identify the do's and don'ts in the relationship between the moderator and the client organization
- to suggest how client organizations can evaluate moderators to determine if they are using the best possible ones.

The Role of the Moderator

The moderator's role in focus group research varies according to the nature of the client organization and the relationship it has established with the moderator. But the prototypical role for the moderator is to manage the implementation of the research process, including preparation, implementation, and analysis.

Preparation

The moderator's responsibilities in preparing for the groups include:

Developing a Proposal. The moderator's proposal should stipulate exactly what his or her responsibilities will be during the research process and what are the costs of these services. This extremely important document ensures that both client and moderator understand exactly what is expected from the moderator.

Developing Research Goals. The moderator should assist the client organization in developing well-thought-out research objectives that are realistic in terms of the capabilities of the focus group methodology.

Determining Participant Criteria. The moderator should work with the client to define the characteristics of the people to be included in the groups, then develop screening criteria that reflect these characteristics so that the correct people are recruited.

Determining Logistics. The moderator should help the client determine the number of groups that are needed to achieve the research objectives, while remaining within the client's budget. He or she should also assist the client in determining the appropriate location(s) for the groups in the light of the research objectives.

Working with the Facility. The moderator should select the best possible research facility to hold the groups and should instruct it about the screening questionnaire, room setup, food requirements (for both participants and clients), and rescreening requirements.

Developing a Moderator Guide. This guide should be based on the client's inputs to the moderator, provided in the briefing meeting, in writing, or over the telephone. Through the first draft of the guide, the moderator shares with the client his or her sense of the content of the focus groups, its information flow, scope, the timing of various topics; and the optimal external stimuli.

Developing External Stimuli. The moderator should help the client decide on the type of external stimuli to be used. If concepts are to be presented, for example, the moderator should suggest ways to expose participants to the concepts to obtain the best output. The moderator should also help the client decide whether pictures should accompany concept statements, whether product prototypes are needed to demonstrate an idea, whether the participants should handle the prototypes, and so on.

Coordinating with the Facility. The moderator should determine well in advance of the groups that recruiting is proceeding on schedule and suggest adjustments in the screening process to ensure that there will be full groups on the day of the sessions. The moderator is also responsible for ensuring that the facility receives an advance payment to cover the co-op payments to the participants.

Implementation

The moderator's most important responsibilities during implementation are:

Arranging Rescreening. The moderator should make arrangements for the facility to rescreen all participants when they arrive to ensure that the right people participate.

Briefing the Observers. The moderator should brief the client personnel who will be observing the groups on the objectives of the group, the contents of the moderator guide, and the various external stimuli that will be used to elicit information from the participants.

Coordinating Interaction with Observers. The moderator should ensure that the observers in the back room understand how he or she will interact with them during the session to gain their inputs. Essentially, this will involve the moderator coming into the back room a few times during the group to talk with the observers.

Conducting the Groups. The moderator should conduct the group so as to cover all the elements in the moderator guide. The moderator can deviate from the guide in the event of a "fertile" topic of discussion, but under no circumstances should the moderator omit parts of the guide that have been agreed upon with the client, without the prior agreement of the client personnel in attendance.

Finishing on Time. The moderator should end the group within ten minutes of the time agreed on with the facility.

After the Groups

The moderator has the following responsibilities after the group has been implemented:

Holding a Briefing. The moderator should conduct a briefing with the people who have observed the session(s) at the end of each day's focus groups. Its purpose is to identify the key issues raised so far in the research process and to enable the observers to share their reactions to the discussions. If the groups are part of a series, the postgroup discussion can help determine changes that should be made in the moderator guide or in the external stimuli for the balance of the groups in the series.

Obtaining Recordings. The moderator should obtain the audio and/or videotapes that were made of the groups and provide a set to the client.

Obtaining Payment Records. The moderator should obtain from the facility the sign-out sheet of all the people who were paid co-op money, as a record of the out-of-pocket expenses that the facility will claim for the sessions.

Key Characteristics of an Effective Moderator

Most successful focus group moderators share some key personal characteristics in common. Some of these characteristics can be learned, but a large number of them are inherited traits that a person either does or does not have. The most important characteristics of successful focus group moderators are as follows.

Natural Characteristics

Superior Listening Ability. It is essential that the moderator be able to listen to what the participants are saying. A moderator must not miss the participants' comments because of lack of attention or misunderstanding. The effective moderator knows how to paraphrase, to restate the comments of a participant when necessary, to ensure that the content of the comments is clear.

Excellent Short-Term Auditory Memory. The moderator must be able to remember comments that participants make early in a group, then correlate them with comments made later by the same or other participants. A participant might say that she rarely watches her weight, for example, then later indicate that she always drinks diet soft drinks. The moderator should remember the first comment and be able to relate it to the later one so that the reason for her diet soft drink consumption is clarified.

Well Organized. The best moderators see things in logical sequence from general to specific and keep similar topics organized together. A good moderator guide should be constructed logically, as should the final report. An effective moderator can keep track of all the details associated with managing the focus group process, so that nothing "falls through the cracks" that impacts negatively on the overall quality of the groups.

A Quick Learner. Moderators become intimately involved in a large number of different subject areas—and for only a very short time in each. An effective moderator is able to learn enough about a subject quickly in order to develop an effective moderator guide and conduct successful group sessions. Moderators normally have only a short period of time to study subject areas about which they will be conducting groups. Therefore, the most effective moderators can identify the key points in any topic area, then focus on them, so that they know enough to listen and/or probe for the nuances that make the difference between an extremely informative and an average group discussion.

High Energy Level. Focus groups can be very boring, both for the participants and for the client observers. When the tenor of a group gets very laid back and lifeless, it dramatically lowers the quality of the information that the participants generate. The best moderators find a way to inject energy and enthusiasm into the group so that both the participants and the observers are energized throughout the session. This ability tends to be most important during the second group of an evening (the eight to ten o'clock session), when observers and participants are frequently tired because of the late hour, and can become listless if they are not motivated to keep their energy and interest levels high. The moderator must be able to keep his or her own energy level high so that the discussion can continue to be very productive to the end.

Personable. The most effective moderators are people who can develop an instant rapport with participants, so that the people become actively involved in the discussion in order to please the moderator. Participants who don't establish rapport with the moderator are much less likely to "open up" during the discussion, and the output from the group is not as good.

Well above Average Intelligence. This is a vital characteristic of the effective moderator, because no one can plan for every contingency that may occur in a focus group session. The moderator must be able to think on his or her feet: to process the information that the group is generating, then determine what line of questioning will most effectively generate further information needed to achieve the research objectives.

Learned Skills

Prior Relevant Business Experience. One of the most important characteristics of an effective moderator (according to the 1990/ 1991 ARF Qualitative Research study) is the ability to do more than simply interpret the results of focus groups. The best moderators have had prior business experience so that they can not only interpret the results but draw conclusions and make recommendations that go well beyond the scope of the groups. It is for this reason that so many marketing consultants and corporate marketing personnel enter the focus group industry: they can offer clients the added value of their practical marketing experience in addition to their interpretative skills.

Category Experience. It is not essential but is is almost always an advantage when a moderator has had some prior experience working in the industry or with the product category about which the research is being conducted. This prior experience enables the moderator to help the client think through the research objectives and the moderator guide more effectively than an inexperienced person could, and it precludes the need to brief the moderator in depth. On the other hand, it can be problematic if the moderator is too much of a category expert, as this can limit his or her objectivity in directing the discussion.

Good Communication. The best focus group moderators are very effective in communicating with others. These communication skills are important to the process of writing the moderator guide, asking questions of the participants during the session, and writing (and perhaps presenting) the final report.

Finding a Moderator

Understanding the characteristics of a good focus group moderator is one thing, but finding moderators who have these skills is normally more difficult. The optimal way to evaluate moderators is to observe groups they conduct, but this is normally not possible due to the confidentiality of focus group research and the fact that most clients do not permit outside observers to watch their sessions.

Watching videos or listening to audiotapes of groups that the moderator has conducted is the best alternative, but this also normally violates client confidentialities. The next best alternative is to obtain several names of clients for whom a moderator has previously worked and talk to them about the moderator. At the same time, reviewing the moderator's resume helps evaluate the person's credentials.

The Moderator-Client Relationship: Do's and Don'ts

This section outlines a series of "do's" and "don'ts" that clients should follow in working with moderators. Following these principles dramatically improves a client's chances of having significantly more effective focus groups.

The Don'ts

Don't Accept Just any Moderator. The client should be very selective when planning focus groups and should not accept as a moderator anyone who is offered to them by a research organization or any moderator who is available in the local market. Nor should the client's project manager be required to use a particular moderator due to internal politics in the company, personal relationships with friends or colleagues, or because the first-choice moderator simply is not available. Choosing a moderator is similar to selecting a physician or dentist: you want to get the very best individual you can, one who will be able to work with you most effectively to achieve your research objectives.

Don't Let Cost Control the Selection of the Moderator. Some client organizations purchase marketing research, particularly focus groups, as if it were a commodity like a bag of sugar or five pounds of flour. But moderating focus groups is a skill that requires a great deal of training and experience to do well, and therefore the cost differences among moderators are legitimate. Generally, the costs of the most and the least expensive vary by only about 25 percent, and in many—if not most—cases, this premium is worth the extra expense. There is normally a reason why a relatively expensive moderator can command more for his or her services than others: the added value this individual brings to the sessions as a result of specific prior experience in the product category, breadth and depth of experience and expertise in moderating, or an established reputation in the qualitative research field. Selecting a moderator based on the lowest bid is like admitting that all moderators are essentially the same and dismissing the concept of "value added."

Don't Treat the Moderator Like an Outsider. The moderator should be considered a member of the project team and therefore should be provided with all the information he or she needs to be effective in the work. Some client organizations give the moderator as little information as possible, for fear that doing so would hurt them some time in the future. As a result, the moderator is not as well prepared as possible for the group discussion and can miss important points that participants make because of a lack of information about the client's research objectives.

Don't Lose Control of the Process. While the moderator can be a great asset to the client organization in effective focus groups, the client's principal contact for the project should be comfortable with all aspects of planning and implementing the groups. This includes agreeing on the screening criteria for the participants, being willing to review and input the moderator guide well in advance of the sessions, and being comfortable with the approach the moderator will take to introducing the concepts or ideas to the participants.

Don't Be Overly Controlling of the Moderator. While it is important for the client contact to be a part of the planning process and to provide input for the moderator guide, one of the biggest mistakes client organizations make is to try to be overcontrolling of the moderator in his or her approach to moderating. The client should select a moderator whom it trusts for his or her professional experience, then permit this individual to execute his or her own procedure—within reasonable guidelines.

Don't Be Reluctant to Challenge the Moderator's Findings, Conclusions, and Recommendations. A good moderator can defend his or her interpretation of all aspects of the group results. If the moderator raises points in the report that conflict with the client's going-in perspective, the client should discuss them with the moderator to learn his or her underlying reasoning. Then it will be possible for the client to decide whether they agree with the moderator's interpretation or discount it as the moderator's perspective, in favor of their own.

The Do's

Take the Time to Find the Right Moderator. Focus groups are often conducted under a very tight timetable, and the selection of a moderator can be heavily dependent on the availability of the candidates. As a result, less qualified moderators are frequently used because they happen to be available on a particular day and the client is unwilling or unable to change the group dates to accommodate the schedule of the first choice moderator.

This significant mistake can be avoided if the client management takes a realistic view of the research schedule. Frequently, a better moderator can be found if the deadline is extended by only a week.

Treat the Moderator as a Member of the Management Team. The moderator should be made privy to any information that will enhance the effectiveness of the focus groups. The moderator should be advised about the anticipated strengths and weaknesses of the concept being evaluated and any legal or environmental questions that might be raised in the group discussions. Also, the moderator should be told about the anticipated performance of the new idea in relation to the competitive entries that will be most familiar to the participants.

As a general rule, the moderator should be provided with any facts about the subject being discussed that will help him or her delve further into the attitudes and motivations of the group participants. If there is any hidden agenda associated with the project, the moderator should be made aware of it before the session, so that it can be considered when planning the research.

Encourage Creativity in the Research Design. Some clients require moderators to follow a very traditional focus group approach and do not permit deviations from it. But some good moderators do not adhere to the traditional approach. Experienced moderators often suggest new ways to accomplish the research objectives that they feel will work well for a project. The client should ask the moderator about any deviation be satisfied that the moderator has thought it through as being an effective way to achieve the research objective. Once this has been accomplished, the client should allow the moderator to proceed with the innovative approach.

Leverage the Moderator's Experience. One major mistake that some clients make is to fail to ask the moderator for his or her interpretation of various things that happen during the groups. Experienced moderators have seen many different types of situations and can often provide a perspective otherwise unavailable to the client. Such a moderator is in a position to compare participants' reactions to the product with reactions to other products discussed in other groups—whether, for example, the reaction to a service was unusually negative in light of its relatively low price. These types of questions the moderator can answer for the client, based on his or her prior experience.

Some moderators also can provide valuable advice about what actions the client organization should take as a result of the conclusions of the research. If he or she has many years' experience in line marketing, for example, or as a strategic marketing consultant, the moderator can offer meaningful advice beyond interpreting the results of the groups.

Evaluating Moderators

Although most users of focus groups agree that having an effective moderator is essential, the ways they commonly assess moderators are normally very subjective. This section provides a series of questions that you should ask yourself about the moderators you use, to determine their overall capabilities and value to your organization. These questions are relevant both for evaluating your existing moderators and for determining whether a new person is appropriate.

What Is the Moderator's Level of Experience? How long has he or she been conducting focus groups, and approximately how many each year? There are many people in the market research industry who are "masquerading" as moderators, who have spent very little time in the industry, and who are using focus groups to build a career in the industry. Just as you would not want to be the first person that a heart surgeon operates on if you needed a bypass, you probably would not want to be a test client for a relatively inexperienced moderator.

Does the Moderator Help Plan the Research Project, or simply Execute the Research the Client Specifies? The better moderators provide assistance to their clients in:

- ensuring that focus groups are the proper methodology to meet the research objectives

- assisting in designing the best possible research program, including determining the most appropriate number of groups, the best participants for them, and the possible need for multiple locations
- helping the client determine the external stimuli that would most effectively elicit information desired from the participants, including working with the client to create concept statements, identifying the need for prototype products to show to the participants, or requesting rough drawings of promotions, new products, or packaging that can be exposed to the participants

Does the Moderator Prepare a Detailed Guide Well in Advance of the Groups? Research has shown that the moderator guide is one of the most important factors in creating a successful focus group project. But some moderators do not feel it is necessary to prepare a detailed guide that covers all the topics to be discussed in the groups and all the techniques to be used to elicit information. Some prefer to work in a completely unstructured environment without the "restrictions" of a guide, while others appear to feel it is unimportant to get substantive client input into the guide.

The importance of a well-constructed moderator guide cannot be over emphasized. It is the best way for the moderator to communicate with the client about the topics that will be covered during the groups and the approximate amount of attention to be given to each. If for no other reason, a moderator guide is vital because it forces the moderator to think through the discussion flow well in advance of the session, minimizing the possibility that key topic areas will be overlooked.

Does the Moderator Adequately Prepare for the Sessions? An effective moderator takes the time to learn enough about the product or service to be able to ask questions of the participants that adequately cover the topics and to hear the nuances of the discussion. Moderators who work as "walk-ons" and moderate focus groups with guides written only by the client and without any meaningful briefing cannot easily maximize the output from the group discussion.

Does the Moderator Offer "Added Value" beyond Moderating the Session? An experienced moderator has the experience to provide clients with meaningful recommendations based on research findings. Having technical knowledge about the product category, or functional experience in marketing, promotion, sales, product development, and the like, makes the difference between merely interesting focus groups and those genuinely helpful in solving the problem for which they have been conceived.

Is the Moderator Up-to-Date on New Techniques in Focus Group Moderation? A number of different techniques for moderating focus groups, some of which are relatively new to the industry are discussed in Chapter 7. Does the moderator use these techniques or others like them when working with the groups? Or has he or she continued to use the same techniques for years?

Does the Moderator Adequately Cover All the Material in the Guide? With some moderators, the last half hour of a session becomes a "catch-up" discussion where it is necessary to rush through the remainder of the guide to cover all the topics. The effective moderator can gauge the time needed for each topic in the guide relatively accurately, so that each is covered in sufficient detail.

Does the Moderator Maintain an Appropriate Balance between Leading the Discussion and Letting It Run Out of Control? Two very different moderator styles are quite problematic. In one, the moderator takes such tight control of the discussion that he or she cannot deviate from the moderator guide, even when an extremely fertile area of discussion comes up. Such moderators tend to lead the participants in the direction they feel the discussion should take in order to please themselves or the client. The other problematic style is that of the moderator who lets the participants determine their own direction and remains very passive during the discussion. Such moderators are not able to adequately cover the material that is desired. An effective moderator will avoid both extremes, keeping the discussion on track, yet allowing for a degree of spontaneity.

Does the Moderator Take Responsibility for Managing the Entire Research Process? Moderators that offer the best overall service to their clients do more than merely moderate the groups. They make all the arrangements for the sessions, including selecting the facility, directing and supervising the facility's recruitment of participants, and arranging for food, props, coop payments, rescreening, and the like.

Does the Moderator Have an Adequate Sense of Urgency about Completing the Project? Some clients find themselves waiting an excessively long time to receive the moderator's final report, causing the research project to lose momentum. As a general rule, the report should be available to the client within seven days of the last group session, or it will lose some of its value. An effective moderator finds out when the client needs the report, then does whatever is necessary to deliver it on the agreed-upon date.

Does the Moderator Have the Energy and Enthusiasm to Keep Participants Interested, Even When the Hour is Late? This is particularly important when conducting two groups in one evening or a series of groups, as it is essential that the moderator be fresh throughout to obtain the maximum output from the participants.

Summary

The moderator is the captain of the ship, the leader of the orchestra and the surgeon with the scalpel all in one. Moderators must be made to feel part of the team throughout the process so that clients can gain the maximum benefit from their involvement in the focus group process. At the same time, it is vital that clients constantly evaluate their current moderators and potential new ones so that the overall quality of the moderators can be at the highest possible level.

Moderator Outline

The Role of the Moderator
   Preparation
      Developing a proposal
      Developing research goals
      Determining participant criteria
      Determining logistics
      Working with the facility

> Developing a moderator guide
> Developing external stimuli
> Coordinating with the facility
>
> Implementation
> > Arranging rescreening
> > Briefing the observers
> > Coordinating interaction with the observers
> > Conducting the groups
> > Finishing on time
>
> After the Groups
> > Holding a briefing
> > Obtaining recordings
> > Obtaining payment records

Key Characteristics of an Effective Moderator
> Natural Characteristics
> > Superior listening ability
> > Excellent short-term auditory memory
> > Well organized
> > A quick learner
> > High energy level
> > Personable
> > Well above average intelligence
>
> Learned skills
> > Prior relevant business experience
> > Category experience
> > Good communication

Finding a Moderator

The Moderator-Client Relationship
> Don'ts
> > Don't accept just any moderator
> > Don't let cost control the selection of the moderator
> > Don't treat the moderator like an outsider
> > Don't lose control of the group process
> > Don't be overly controlling of the moderator
> > Don't be reluctant to challenge the moderator's analysis
>
> Do's
> > Take time to find the right moderator
> > Treat the moderator as a member of the management team
> > Encourage creativity in the research design

Leverage the moderator's experience
Evaluating Moderators
   Level of experience
   Level of participation in planning
   Preparation of moderator guide
   Adequacy of preparation
   "Added value"
   Awareness of new techniques
   Adequacy of coverage of guide contents
   Control of group balanced with spontaneity
   Level of responsibility accepted
   Sense of urgency
   Level of energy and enthusiasm

6

Controlling the Costs of Focus Group Research

This chapter is about money—and how clients can keep the costs of focus group research as low as possible, without sacrificing quality. The cost of focus group research has recently become an increasingly important issue in the research community. One reason for this is the continuing pressure on all organizations, profit or nonprofit, to keep marketing and sales-related costs down, especially expenditures (such as research) that do not *directly* increase revenues. Another reason is that most organizations' market research budgets have not been increasing as much as marketing personnel would like, so that the effectiveness of the research that is implemented must be maximized. The purpose of this chapter is to identify the various costs involved in focus group research, then to suggest ways that clients can minimize them.

The Costs of Focus Group Research

In order to effectively control the expense of focus groups, it is necessary to understand the different costs involved in them. Understanding all the factors that contribute to the cost of focus groups will help clients decide where they can comfortably reduce the cost of their focus groups.

Focus group costs can be divided into six general categories.

1. Facility Costs

These are the principal costs a focus group facility charges for the use of its offices and the implementation of the group sessions. The facility is generally one of hundreds of independent market research companies throughout the United States that provide a variety of services to moderators that enable them to conduct their research. The principal services for which a facility charges its clients are:

Room Rental. The facility charges a rental fee that covers both the focus group room and the observation room, connected to each other by a one-way mirror. Room rentals vary considerably based on the location of the facility and the size of the rooms. Some facilities charge different rates according to the time of day, since there is less demand for daytime than for evening sessions; rates may also depend on the number of groups that are conducted in a series or the number of sessions that are implemented in a day at the location. Other facilities give discounts based on ongoing usage of the facility (that is, heavy users pay less per group), or if a research project uses more than one facility location owned by the same company.

Food for the Participants. The cost of food at focus groups can be significant, depending on what is served. The food can range from simple items such as deli sandwiches (the most common) to very elaborate meals, which some clients feel they must provide to attract certain target segments to the sessions. Some groups are conducted at a time of day that does not require any significant food, and small items such as doughnuts, cookies, soft drinks, and coffee are sufficient.

Food for the Client Observers. As with the food provided to the participants, many options are available for the food served to the observers in the back room. Some clients demand elaborate meals with plenty of wine and liquor, whereas others are satisfied with simple fare such as pizza, Chinese food, or deli sandwiches. The cost differences between the various alternatives can be considerable and definitely should be considered in the overall planning.

Extra Services Requested of the Facility. Some clients simply arrive at a focus group, oversee the proceedings while eating a light meal, then depart. Others expect the facility to offer many different services while they are there. It is not unusual for a client to request that multiple copies of various documents be made, whether for use during the session with the participants or for any other reason. Most facilities charge ten or fifteen cents per page for copying. Sometimes a facility is asked to purchase competitive product samples to be used as props during the sessions. Facilities normally charge on an hourly basis for the time their people must spend shopping for the product. Long-distance telephone calls are another extra service that facilities provide and charge for.

Videotaping. If the client chooses to videotape the sessions, the extra costs incurred can amount to as much as $350 per group. Some facilities do not charge for videotaping, whereas others charge one fee for a fixed camera, with no camera operator, and another when a professional is brought in to handle the camera.

Hostesses. Another significant cost element is the expense of having people at the facility to greet the participants, serve the food, and handle the needs of the client observers.

2. Participant Costs

Recruiting costs are the expenses incurred in finding the correct people to participate in the groups. They fall into two major components.

Recruitment Costs. This is the expense associated with making telephone calls to find people (based on the screening questionnaire) who are willing to participate in the sessions. The cost of recruiting participants varies dramatically based on the relative difficulty of finding people who meet the recruiting criteria *and* are willing to participate.

Co-op Costs. These are the fees paid to the participants for their time and for personal expenses associated with coming to the session. The amount that participants are paid depends on a variety of factors, such as:

- the time of day of the session
- the difficulty of finding qualified people based on the recruiting criteria (for example, difficult-to-reach people are paid a higher co-op than others, to ensure their presence)

- the income level of the participants
- the job classification of the people: whether they are housewives, professionals, children, physicians, and so on.

3. Moderator Costs

The costs that relate to the moderator include the following:

Moderator Fee. This is the fee the moderator charges to conduct the focus groups. The amount will depend on:

- *The experience and "value added" that the moderator brings to the sessions.* Moderator fees vary widely based on this factor. Some moderators command significantly higher fees than others because of their level of experience in qualitative research generally or because they have expertise in the specific topic area.
- *The amount of preparation the moderator requires.* If the topic to be discussed is very complex, the moderator may have to spend extra time (and therefore charge a higher fee) to learn enough to be effective.
- *The number of groups in the series.* The cost per group normally declines as the number of sessions increases.
- *The number of groups conducted each day.* The cost per group will almost always be less for groups conducted in one day than for two. Some moderators will conduct as many as four groups in a day, and typically charge less per session than they would in one, for two.
- *The location of the groups.* Travel requires more of the moderator's time, which translates into higher costs.

The Final Report. Moderator costs often depend heavily on the nature of the final report that the client expects. It can vary from no report at all to a simple three-to-five-page top-line summary, to a very elaborate, detailed analysis. The cost of the report varies considerably because the time required to prepare each alternative varies considerably.

Presentation of the Report. At the conclusion of the research project, some clients are satisfied to receive the moderator's report in the mail. Others demand a stand-up presentation of the results. The moderator cost can vary significantly in this respect.

4. External Stimuli Costs

Many focus group sessions use external stimuli to generate the maximum output from the participants. An external stimulus can be something as simple as a competitive product sample or an add cut out from a magazine; or it can be quite elaborate, involving the development of original advertising, product prototypes, or actual working models of the item being evaluated. Depending on the needs in this area, the costs can vary considerably.

5. Travel Costs

A major expense for focus group research is the cost of travel, which may include airfare, hotels, and meals. Sometimes the travel cost is the largest single component of the focus group expenses, particularly if the client must fly several people to multiple cities to observe the sessions. Travel expenses can be so considerable that some client organizations require moderators to be located in the same city as the facility and permit only one or two people from the company to observe sessions outside the home market.

6. Soft Costs

A major expense that is almost never planned for in advance is the "soft costs" associated with the project—the cost of the time that the client personnel spend in preparing for or observing the sessions. Most organizations do not consider this cost an expense for research since the people are already on the company payroll and are paid their salary regardless of their involvement in the specific project. But some organizations do recognize the value of their employees' time and therefore allocate a "memo" cost for their involvement with the research.

The Range of Costs

What follows is a rough estimate of the various expenses that a client can expect to incur for the various aspects of focus group research. These cost estimates are based on the 1991 rates for typical facilities in major metropolitan areas. Focus groups held outside large cities will normally cost significantly less than groups held in major metropolitan areas.

Group 1: Facility Costs

As shown in table 6–1, the range of facility costs varies considerably, from a low of $600 per session to a high of $1,400. The largest component is normally the room rental charge.

Group 2: Recruiting Costs

The recruiting of participants involves identifying people who qualify for the group (based on the screening criteria) and paying co-op fees to the participants. The costs of recruiting range very significantly based on the location of the group and the cost structure of different recruiting organizations. The table 6–2 provides an overview of typical recruiting and co-op costs, assuming twelve people are recruited to get a group of ten respondents. (We overrecruit by two people on the assumption that some will not show up.)

Group 3: Moderation Costs

One of the major costs of focus group research is the charges associated with the moderator. These costs vary widely according to the moderator's training, experience, and special expertise.

Table 6–3 summarizes the estimated range of costs that modera-

TABLE 6–1
Range of Facility Costs for a Ten-Person Group

Cost Element	High	Low	Explanation
Room rental	$ 600	$250	per group
Food for participants	20	10	deli platter/per person
Food for client observers	25	10	deli platter/per person
Videotaping	350	150	with operator*
Total	$1,400	$600	

*Some facilities do not charge for videotaping when no operator is used.

TABLE 6–2

Range of Costs for Recruiting Twelve Participants ($)

Type of participant	Recruiting Cost High	Recruiting Cost Low	Co-Op Fees High	Co-Op Fees Low
Adult consumer of commonly used product	900	500	75	30
Adult consumer of relatively low-incidence product (10 percent or less incidence)	1,400	1,000	100	50
Industrial middle manager, average-incidence product	1,100	900	75	50
Professional (e.g., physician, architect, lawyer)	1,400	1,100	150	75
High-level corporate executive	1,400	1,000	200	100
Teenage consumer of average-incidence product	900	650	40	25

tors charge for conducting the groups, writing the report, and providing a formal presentation of the results. These costs can vary by as much as $11,000 for a series of six focus groups, including a full report and a formal presentation.

Group 4: External Stimuli Costs

The costs of external stimuli can be relatively insignificant, in the case of single concept boards, or very meaningful if more complex

TABLE 6–3

Range of Moderator Costs, for Six Groups

Service	Range High	Range Low	Comments/Explanation
Moderation	$1,500	$300	per group
Report writing	3,000	500	assumes full report
Formal presentation	1,500	250	assumes half day at client office to present the report
Total	$13,500	$2,550	

stimuli are used. Table 6–4 summarizes the cost range for several different types of external stimuli.

Groups 5 and 6: Travel and "Soft Costs"

Both the travel and the "soft costs" associated with focus group research vary significantly. The most important factors are the number of people and amount of time involved in planning for the group, preparing the moderator guide, and developing various external stimuli. Another major cost element is the number of people who travel to the groups to observe the sessions, particularly if air travel is required.

Reducing the Costs

Now that you have a good understanding of the various costs involved in focus group research, you can consider taking various actions to reduce the costs. This section provides a series of suggestions that could save you significant amounts of money without sacrificing the quality of the research.

Tip 1: Ensure That the Research Is Really Needed

The biggest cost savings you can realize is to decide that you really *do not* need to conduct focus groups. Because of the current pop-

TABLE 6–4

Range of External Stimuli Costs (per item)

External Stimulus	High	Low	Comments/Explanation
Concept boards—no artwork	$ 50	nothing	No cost assumes photocopying; high cost assumes typesetting
Concept boards—artwork	1,000	$100	
Advertising storyboards	5,000	500	
Prototype print ad	2,500	500	
Packaging comp	2,500	250	
Wooden product model	$5,000	$500	

ularity of the focus group technique, marketing persons commonly jump to the conclusion that focus groups are the appropriate technique to use when questions need to be answered, decisions have to be made, or information needs to be obtained. You might consider asking yourself the following before you undertake focus group research:

- What would be the risk of making the decision without the benefit of research? Is the cost of doing the research worth the value of the information?
- Is the type of information you are seeking already available from some other source, such as an existing research study lying in the company files or secondary sources?
- What is the likelihood that you will be able to learn what you need from focus groups? Will the participants be able **and** willing to provide you with the information? Many participants do not wish to share their views in a group environment, especially on topics such as sexual preference, sexual behavior, incontinence, constipation, or problems with children or spouses. Other participants are not able to share their knowledge with a group, such as confidential information about their business. Still others simply do not know the information that you are trying to obtain, such as their electricity costs, annual car repair costs, how much money they spent on clothes last year, or the number of batteries they use in toys and appliances. Since most people have only a vague idea about such matters, a focus group may not produce the information needed.
- Will the client's key decision-makers accept the results of the research even if they are not consistent with their going-in biases?

Each of these questions should be asked before you commit funds for focus groups, as the answer to any of them might mean focus groups are inappropriate or unnecessary.

Tip 2: Keep the Number of Groups as Low as Possible

The costs of focus group research increases almost proportionately with the number of groups in a series. Six groups are almost half again as expensive as four, while ten groups cost almost double the cost of five.

In my experience, many organizations conduct far more focus groups than they really need to meet their research objectives. Groups are frequently over scheduled when researchers or clients feel they need to "cover all the bases" by holding groups among several market segments in multiple geographic areas. Consider the following questions when planning a focus group project:

- Do you really need to go to multiple geographic areas? Are the responses in different locations likely to be sufficiently different that they will affect your *decision making?*
- Do you really need to talk to all of the target groups that you have identified, or can you get by with eliminating one or two?
- Do you really need to do more than two groups in each market to get the information you need?

Tip 3: Simplify the Screening Criteria as Much as Possible

Insisting on very specific screening criteria that the recruiters cannot violate will significantly increase the cost of finding qualified participants. This is not to suggest that you should be lax about the screening criteria—it is absolutely essential to have the right participants in the room.

But sometimes a client's screening criteria are so complex that the overall costs increase dramatically because the people who qualify are so hard to find or, once located, are not willing to participate in focus group research. It is much more difficult to find people who have used three specific laundry detergent brands in the past six months, for example, than people who use one brand but have tried the others in the past two years. Similarly, insisting on participants who are all financial vice-presidents of Fortune 100 companies is much more expensive than those of the Fortune 1000. Although companies frequently want to do focus groups with CEOs of Fortune 500 companies, experience has shown that it is almost impossible to convince these people to participate in focus groups— at any price. Therefore, you should determine whether you *really* need a CEO, or whether another high-ranking person in the organization would be sufficient to meet your research objectives.

In summary, the more complex the screening criteria are, the more expensive the recruitment process will be. The more difficult the people are to find, the more valuable they are and the higher their co-op costs will have to be. It is therefore important to think through the screening criteria very carefully to ensure that their detail and complexity are really necessary. Making a minor change in the screening criteria can often result in significant financial savings.

Tip 4: Carefully Monitor the Amount of the Co-op Payment

Co-op payments to participants are a necessary evil of focus group research. In fact, focus groups—and one-on-ones—are the only commonly used research techniques in which the participants are paid. Unfortunately, co-op payments are one of the largest cost components in focus groups. Moreover, co-op payments are the one part of the process where the client and the facility generally are at odds. The client normally wants to keep the co-op payment as low as possible to minimize its research costs, while the facility has an interest in paying as high a co-op as possible so that qualified participants will be more likely to agree to take part. Offering a higher co-op lowers their cost of recruiting and therefore increases the overall profitability of the project for them.

In light of these conflicting objectives, the client must ensure that the co-op that the facility suggests is really what is needed to motivate participants to come, rather than a larger amount that will make the recruiting easier for the facility. The difference can be meaningful relative to the total cost of the research. A focus group of twelve professionals that offers a $75 co-op per participant, for example, will cost $300 less than one that pays $100 (twelve people times $25). For a series of six groups, this can amount to a total savings of $1,800.

Tip 5: Keep the Moderator Costs as Low as Possible

Taking advantage of several controllable moderator costs can result in significantly less expensive focus groups. This is not to suggest that focus group moderating should be treated like a commodity and that the lowest bidder should be chosen. As discussed in Chapter 5; there are *dramatic* differences among moderators in their skills in conducting groups, in their ability to write effective reports, and in the "value added" they bring to a research project.

Nonetheless, the cost of the moderator portion of focus group research can be significantly reduced by considering the following:

Use One or Two Moderators Regularly. A moderator who does many groups for your company will likely give you a much more favorable rate, due to your overall importance to them as a valuable client. Many moderators offer their clients discounts based on the number of groups they do for a client over a period of time, such as 5 percent off after the first twenty-five groups, 10 percent after fifty, and so on.

Use the Moderator's Time Sparingly. Do not utilize more than is absolutely needed, either before or after the groups. Some clients want moderators to spend considerable time before the groups are held listening to the inputs of many people about the topic to be covered. Sometimes, to be sure, there is a real need to give the moderator varied perspectives from many people in the company. At other times, extensive discussions with many people are held solely for reasons of internal politics, to ensure that nobody is left out of the process who could be a problem later on.

For the final report, some organizations demand that the moderator make several presentations to different constituencies, so that each of them is aware of the progress of the project. It is certainly often desirable to keep many different people informed, but many moderators charge clients based on the time they spend on the project. Heavy demands on the moderator's time before and after the groups can add significant costs to the overall study.

Keep the Report Simple. Do not ask the moderator to write a more detailed report than is absolutely necessary.

In many situations, a "top line" summary is adequate, and a long and detailed analysis is unnecessary. Writing the report is often the most time-consuming part of the focus group process. If no detailed analysis or even a report is necessary, doing without it can result in meaningful cost savings.

Schedule the Sessions Close Together. Try to combine sessions into a concentrated time frame, to maximize the utilization of the moderator's time. Moderators normally charge less per group when three are scheduled in one day than if two are planned. Above all, avoid doing only one group in one day. Most moderators charge almost as much to do one group as two, since they put in as much time before and after the session (planning and analyzing), and the only difference is the additional two hours at the facility for the second group.

Tip 6: Question the Necessity of Videotapes

Some organizations routinely videotape groups to have a visual record for their files. While this is sometimes helpful, my experience is that most focus group videotapes are never viewed. Since the cost of videotaping (particularly with a camera operator) can be as high as $350 per group, you should be sure that videotaping is really necessary.

Tip 7: Monitor the Food Costs

The food provided to the participants and the client observers can represent a significant cost if you are not careful to control it. The food served to the clients is more significant here, as participants are usually given very simple fare like deli sandwiches. But some clients use focus groups as an opportunity for gourmet dining and ask the facility to prepare an elaborate meal for the observers. I recall one client who demanded a very large bowl of fresh shrimp and a side of crab legs as an appetizer before an evening of focus group sessions. This added several hundred dollars to the cost of the research, which had to be passed on to the client organization. Other clients I have worked with want to impress the participants, who are also their customers, by serving elaborate meals with crystal, china, and waitress service rather than the traditional deli platter. This can add $500 to $1,000 to the cost of each group.

Tip 8: Invite Only Essential People to Out-of-Town Groups

The soft costs and the travel and entertainment expenses associated with out-of-town groups can be a major cost element, yet most companies do not consider this when planning a budget for focus group research. I have seen clients transport up to six people to several different cities just to sit in the back room and observe the proceedings. One or two client people are often necessary in order to interact with the moderator in various discussions before, during, and after the groups, but more are rarely necessary. They can view a videotape rather than spend the client's time and money traveling to the sessions.

Summary

Most experts in the market research industry agree that the costs of focus groups will continue to increase over the next several years, probably at rates that far exceed inflation. This chapter identified various cost factors in focus group research, then provided tips for reducing the costs. Following these suggestions can help you significantly lower the cost of focus group research.

Cost Control Outline

The Costs of Focus Group Research
  Facility Costs
    Room rental
    Food for participants
    Food for client observers
    Extra services requested
    Videotaping
    Hostesses
  Participant Costs
    Recruitment Costs
    Co-op costs
  Moderator Costs
    Moderator fee
    The final report
    Presentation of the report
  External Stimuli Costs
  Travel Costs
  Soft Costs

The Range of Costs

Reducing the Costs
    Insure that research is really needed
    Keep the number of groups as low as possible
    Simplify the screening criteria as much as possible
    Carefully monitor the amount of co-op
    Keep the moderator costs as low as possible
        Use one or two moderators regularly
        Use the moderator's time sparingly
        Keep the report simple
        Schedule the sessions close together
    Question the necessity of videotapes
    Monitor the food costs
    Invite only essential people to out-of-town groups

7

New Moderating Techniques

The focus group industry has been in transition since the technique became popular in the 1970s. Many leading moderators have developed innovative techniques to distinguish themselves from others in the field and to improve the overall quality of their research. This chapter overviews some of the new techniques that have been developed in recent years. Due to the large number of moderators today, it would be impossible to cover all or even most of the new techniques. Hence I have chosen to describe the techniques that I feel are most useful to most moderators working now.

The techniques discussed in this chapter fall into three different categories:

- projective techniques
- probing techniques
- control techniques

These different techniques grew out of differing approaches to the use of external stimuli. In focus groups generally, moderators often use external stimuli to stimulate reactions, especially product prototypes, advertising storyboards, new product concept statements, and packaging samples. Generally, moderators attempt to elicit the following types of reactions from focus group participants:

- their overall reaction to the product, concept, or package, whether positive or negative
- the key copy points for the advertising, packaging, and new product concept

- their concerns about the concept or prototype, and their suggestions as to what make it more appealing to them
- their intention to purchase the product or service.

All of these are very important areas of discussion in focus group sessions, and the discussions can generate information that is very useful in achieving the client's research objectives. But all of these areas of discussion focus on very concrete and specific reactions—reactions that participants could just as easily have written down on a quantitative questionnaire. A moderator who seeks to obtain such reactions alone is not leveraging the specific benefit of the focus group technique—that is its ability to have a two-way dialogue between the moderator and the participants in which they can delve deeper than simply responding to an interviewer's question. Moderating approaches that foster such two-way dialogues are the projective techniques and the probing techniques: Both are designed to stimulate participants to share more of their feelings about the subject being discussed than they normally would on a questionnaire or even with traditional moderating techniques. Control techniques are those that seek to maximize the benefits and minimize the limitations of group dynamics by properly controlling them.

Projective Techniques

Projective techniques are a group of focus group moderating tools that generate information from participants by encouraging them to make associations with other stimuli as a way of expressing their feelings toward the specific conceptual idea, product, service, or other entity with which they are being presented. Essentially, these techniques evoke reactions to a familiar stimulus in order to help people share their feelings about a new one. They are not unlike the ink blot tests that psychologists use to get their patients to express their innermost feelings. How a psychologist interprets patients' comments is much more complicated than how a moderator interprets participants' comments, but the principle is the same: They both use a secondary stimulus to elicit the individual's feelings. Six kinds of projective techniques are sometimes used in focus group moderating:

- personality associations
- situational associations

- forced relationships
- sentence completions
- expressive drawing
- anthropomorphization

Personality Associations

The personality association technique uses photographs to stimulate the participants' thinking and help them articulate their feelings about the topic being discussed. This technique works extremely well for both adult and children's focus groups. Personality association techniques may be either "fixed" or "variable," depending on how the photographs are used.

Variable Personality Associations. In variable personality associations, the moderator uses a series of photographs of people to stimulate group discussion. These can be pictures of people without any special background, or the people in them may be involved in specific situations such as walking, loving, buying or talking. What makes this technique "variable" is that the photos are chosen based on the topic of discussion.

For a focus group that is exploring feelings of women toward a new type of household cleaner, for example, a series of photos might be used that show women in different domestic environments and in different moods. One picture might show a woman who looks proud because of the end result of using the product; another might show a woman getting the praise of her friends or family; a third might show an exhausted woman who has just completed the household task she dislikes the most; and a fourth might show a woman dissatisfied with the task she has just completed.

The moderator then asks the participants to share their feelings as to which of the women is a user of the new product being discussed in the group. This can give important insights into the participants' feelings toward the product because people tend to *project* their own feelings into the pictures of the women. If they feel (or think they would feel) happy because they used the product, their association would be with the happy women. Similarly, if they felt the product was easy to use, they would choose the photos of satisfied women.

Most moderators who use this approach feel that it is normally better to tailor the photos to the specific topic, in order to have more control over the input generated by the group discussion. For example, using the technique to explore participants' attitudes toward kitchen appliances works best when the pictures are in a kitchen environment. Similarly, for a group intended to explore the service in a retail store, the pictures should focus on that environment.

The key to the successful use of the variable personality association technique is to select the photos with great care, to ensure that they provide a wide range of options to the participants. It is all the more productive when the moderator probes the participants in depth about why they relate to the specific photos they have chosen.

Fixed Personality Associations. In the fixed personality association technique, one set of photos is established and this same set is always used. The photos are selected according to specific characteristics of the people they represent, such as different groups of adults, different groups of children, blue-collar men, athletes, and so on. What distinguishes this "fixed" approach from the variable one is that once the set of photos has been established, it does not change, since consistency of the photos is the key to the technique.

As a moderator uses these pictures over an extended period of time, he or she becomes very familiar with consumer reactions to each of them. Each person in the photographs develops a "personality profile" over time, based on comments that participants in various focus groups make about that person. The moderator can use this "personality profile" during a group to probe certain areas with the participants. If a man in one of the photographs has developed the profile of being very sophisticated and extremely educated, yet some participants in a group see him as a very unsophisticated person, the moderator would explore the feelings of these people in greater depth in an attempt to understand their reasons. Such fixed picture associations can give a moderator much more insight into the participants' attitudes than is usually possible with variable picture associations.

The People Board as we have come to call it, shown in Figure 7–1, has been used in hundreds of focus groups to obtain the feelings of participants toward various institutions, products, promotions, and services. It contains a fixed series of photos of different types of people, each designated by a letter of the alphabet from A to S. Two examples of how this device is used are as follows:

Research Objective: Develop a Profile of a Retail Bank. A focus group is conducted to gain insight into the feelings of customers and noncustomers toward a particular retail bank. The People Board is used to elicit the feelings of the participants about the types of people who do and do not do their banking there. Each participant is provided with an input sheet (see Figure 7–2), on which they are asked to circle the letter or letters from A to S that correspond to the person(s) depicted on the People Board who **"definitely do"** and **"definitely do not"** bank with the subject institution. The participants are told that they can circle as many (or as few) people as they feel are appropriate. The participants are given five minutes to study the photos and record their answers on the tally sheet.

When the participants complete the written exercise, the moderator writes down the letters A to S on the easel. Then he goes through the letters one by one to find the number of people who indicated "definitely yes" and "definitely no" about each People Board person's relationship. As a result of this tabulation exercise, the moderator generates several results:

- A sense of the perceived differences between people who do and do not bank with the institution. Similar tabulation exercises are used to determine the People Board people who are perceived as definitely using or not using particular product brands and services. In my experience, the People Board exercise almost always identifies a few people on the board who most of the participants feel definitely do and do not represent the product or service's target consumers. This information can help the moderator develop a profile of the users and nonusers of the product or service.
- The opportunity to ask the participants why they feel various People Board people do and do not bank with the selected institution. Since the participants have already identified specific People Board people as customers and noncustomers, it is relatively easy to get them to articulate why they feel that way.
- A vehicle for playing the feelings of one participant against those of another, to delve further into the reasons for their

(Circle Those That Are Appropriate)

DEFINITELY YES		DEFINITELY NO
A		A
B		B
C		C
D		D
E		E
F		F
G		G
H		H
I		I
J		J
K		K
L		L
M		M
N		N
O		O
P		P
Q		Q
R		R
S		S

FIGURE 7–1

The People Board (above)

FIGURE 7–2

People Board Exercise

reactions. Asking a participant who feels that individual Q is a customer to explain her rationale to a participant who feels that Q is not a customer can give rise to some very interesting discussion. As with many other focus group techniques, the more interaction there is among the participants (with minimal moderator intervention), the more effective the group session is likely to be in generating meaningful and helpful inputs.

The effective use of this fixed personality association technique can give the moderator excellent insight into the perceived personality of the bank (and perhaps that of its major competition) and of the types of people who are regarded as being the bank's customers. Both these inputs can be very important to the bank's marketing and communications people in planning marketing programs to obtain new accounts for the institution, developing new advertising, creating new services, and the like.

Research Objective: To Obtain Consumer Reactions to a Retail Store Promotion. A series of focus groups is held to identify consumer reactions to a proposed promotion that a major retail chain is considering to build customer loyalty and ultimately increase sales volume. The moderator understands that consumers normally do not admit that *they* respond positively to "gimmicks" like promotions. So she uses the People Board to identify the strengths and weaknesses of the proposed promotion. She presents the participants with the promotional idea in the form of a concept board and asks them to identify the people on the People Board who *definitely will* and *definitely will not* respond to the promotion. This is accomplished using the same data collection sheets discussed in the retail bank example. Once she records the information on the easel, the moderator can discuss the following types of information with the participants.

- The types of people who will and will not respond to the promotion. If the promotion does appeal to the participants in the group, the fixed personality association technique identifies (or at least provides insight into) the types of people who will respond to them. If, however, the promotion is not of interest to the participants, it is reflected in their profiling of the types of people who are interested.

- Once the people are identified that will and will not respond to the promotion, the moderator ascertains the reasons why the participants feel people will respond the way they will.

The personality association technique generates excellent information about participants' reactions to a specific topic, in a way that is completely nonthreatening to them. Further, because there are both fixed and variable approaches, moderators can adapt the one that most closely meets their needs.

Situational Associations

Situational associations are very similar to personality associations in that they too employ pictures to stimulate responses from the participants. But the pictures used in situational associations emphasize people in specific situations, as well as different places and things, rather than specific types of people. Some of the photos do not even have humans in the picture at all.

A Caribbean resort, for example, might use this technique for a focus group to identify the most appropriate positioning for its "high season" advertising. The resort offers prospective vacationers such benefits as golf, tennis, swimming, fishing, great food, excellent service, tourist attractions, and much more, but the advertising campaign must focus on only one or two of these if it is to have the desired impact. Therefore, a focus group is conducted to assist in this positioning effort. It uses situational associations to ascertain which benefits hold the most attraction for the participants to help this resort compete more effectively with other resorts for the customer's vacation dollar. Obviously, in this situation the individual interests of the participants will significantly affect their reactions (tennis players will respond more favorably to a picture of a tennis court than of a golf course; fishermen will be more interested in fishing than in tennis or golf) so the participants must be screened with great care.

In the sessions, a series of photos is presented to participants showing vacationers in different situations in the resort, such as relaxing by the ocean, having breakfast on the balcony in their hotel room, getting superlative service from a hotel employee, or visiting an exciting tourist attraction near the hotel. The participants are asked to name which situation corresponds most closely to their wishes for their winter vacation, and which does not correspond at all.

This technique generates several potential discussion topics for the group. One of these is an assessment of the types of situations that appeal and those that do not appeal to the participants. This will give insights into their vacation needs and the trade-offs they are willing to make between service, cost, sightseeing availability nearby, outstanding golf or tennis facilities, and so on.

Another topic of discussion is the reasons why the situations shown do and do not appeal to the participants. Perhaps of greatest importance, the participants can discuss what "ideal" resort experience is not shown in any of the photos at all. Some vacationers, for example, may not even consider a resort that does not have a well-stocked exercise facility. If this is shown in none of the photos and alluded to in none of the advertising copy, such a consumer could bring up this omission during the discussion. The moderator would then assess how important it is to the other participants in the group. Other participants might have negative reactions to pictures of people enjoying themselves at a local amusement park. A well-orchestrated focus group using situational analysis could determine that they see the pictures as conveying a "honky-tonk" environment or an intention to cater to families with young children. The client organization would then weigh this input in terms of its marketing and target audience objectives.

In summary, situational projectives help the participants express feelings that they might not otherwise articulate. This technique also enables the client to expose a very specific concept (like horse-back riding) to the participants to determine its appeal to consumers both in the absolute and relative to other concepts that the client might want to feature in its promotional program.

Forced Relationships

Forced relationships are probably the oldest projective technique used by focus group moderators; they are also the most nondirective of the commonly used projective techniques. In a forced relationship projective the participants are asked to indicate which of several images in a category most closely relate to the subject being discussed. The categories that are most commonly used are automobiles, colors, and animals, since these appear to have a specific meaning to virtually all consumers and because consumers are normally familiar with a large number of them and therefore can make definite choices when asked.

Animals. Animals are used in forced relationship exercises as follows. Suppose the marketing director of a financial institution is trying to gain insight into the image of the organization. The focus group moderator might ask the participants to write on a piece of paper the name of the animal that they most closely associate with the financial institution and why they selected this particular animal. Some participants at first react to this type of exercise with a reasonably negative attitude, feeling that it is silly. But most of the time they find the exercise to be fun and it generates very interesting perspectives about the topic being discussed.

In virtually every case, the animal that a participant chooses represents an expression of that person's feelings toward the financial institution, perhaps even without the individual's awareness of the fact. Some examples, with their relevant associations, are:

- *Bear*—often associated with caring organizations, ones that are large and friendly
- *Lion*—as the king of the jungle, it is normally associated with very strong organizations that have great power. Normally, organizations associated with lions are not seen as being as friendly as "bear" organizations.
- *Racehorse (or greyhound dog)*—often given to very sleek and streamlined organizations that are very efficient but not necessarily friendly or particularly powerful. Often, they refer to an organization that is quite prestigious, particularly if the racehorse is a stallion or well-known horse.
- *Snake, reptile, or rodent*—normally very negative associations, indicating a nontrusting feeling about the institution. These animals are not particularly friendly and are quite unpredictable; organizations associated with these animals tend to be perceived as such.
- *Turtle*—often refer to very slow-moving, backward organizations.

The types of animals that the participants select will give the moderator insight into the group's overall feelings toward the topic being discussed. The more a moderator uses projective techniques like this, the more familiar he or she will become with the meanings of the various animals and how to use the group dynamics to interpret them.

In the second and perhaps more important part of this exercise, the moderator asks the participants to share with the group *why* they selected the animal they did. This enables the moderator (and the observers) to benefit directly from the participants' own interpretations of their selections. Experienced moderators will probe each participant to learn as much as possible about their association between the financial institution and the animal they chose. They will also explore why they reject animals selected by other participants. Forced relationship techniques are normally used in one of two situations: First, when the participants are having difficulty (in the judgment of the moderator) articulating their feelings toward the topic. The topic may be relatively mundane or uninteresting to them (like toilet bowl cleaners, shoe polish, or checking accounts), thus detracting from their motivation to participate actively in the discussion.

The second situation is one where the moderator feels there is a need to energize the group. Sometimes discussions get stale because the participants are tired due to the late hour. Introducing a forced relationship exercise can add new energy to the session and increase both the quality and quantity of the output.

Animals are probably the most commonly used category for forced relationship exercises. Two other categories are frequently used and deserve some discussion. They are colors and cars.

Colors. Colors are probably the easiest of the three categories to use, but are also riskiest in terms of obtaining meaningful, fresh, high-quality input. Participants generally have no difficulty associating a color and a particular product or service, but there is a danger that their color selection will be greatly influenced by the advertising or packaging of the research topic. In a color exercise about IBM, for example, a disproportionate number of participants are likely to indicate the color blue because of IBM's well-known blue-

and-white logo. A color exercise would probably not provide much meaningful insight in this case, since the participants would probably indicate that they selected blue because of the logo. Similarly, participants asked to provide a color association with Arm & Hammer baking soda are inordinately likely to name yellow, since the product's yellow box is widely familiar.

Color associations are best used for products and services that have no colors strongly tied to them. When colors are used in forced relationship exercises, some of their connotations could be:

- hot colors (red, orange, violet)—warm, friendly
- cold colors (blue, green)—less friendly, distant
- black—distant, mysterious, upscale, sleek
- white—honest, pure, feminine
- pastel colors—feminine
- deep colors—masculine, sophisticated, expensive

But these associations are by no means ironclad, and in this exercise it is crucial to explore the participants' reasons for their selections.

Automobiles. As with colors and animals, the participants are asked what automobile they most commonly associate with a particular product or service. Automobiles are a very helpful category to use in groups of men, particularly men under thirty-five years of age. Such people tend to relate very well to cars and normally have a distinct image of the images that various cars convey and the types of people who drive them. Associating cars with the product or service can often work better for such men than direct questioning does.

The limitations of the color exercise in its use for products or services that already have color images also apply to automobiles. The moderator must ensure that the product or service being evaluated has not recently conducted an advertising program or other promotion that featured a specific brand of automobile.

In summary, forced relationship projective techniques can work very well to elicit information from participants. They are normally not written into the guide, as most moderators decide to use them when circumstances call for them: when participants are having difficulty articulating their feelings or seem to need energizing. The moderator must ensure that the category selected (colors, animals, cars) has no preexisting associations with the product that will influence the participants' choices.

Sentence Completions

Another type of projective technique frequently used in focus groups is sentence completions. In these, the participants are presented with a series of partially completed statements and are asked to provide the rest. Like other projectives, sentence completions can help moderators delve further into the participants' minds in order to learn more about their feelings and motivations.

Sentence completions are normally used in one of three circumstances. One is, when the research topic is not inherently interesting, requiring external stimuli to generate discussion. Another, perhaps the more common use, is when the moderator wishes to explore specific aspects of the product that might not otherwise come up for discussion.

A third is a situation in which participants might normally have difficulty talking about a topic and therefore an assist is needed. In this case the sentence completion exercise can be very helpful since the moderator can construct a sentence that will direct the nature of the discussion to a specific topic.

Sentence completions were effectively used for a client that was developing a new light wine. The research was implemented to explore consumer feelings toward a wine with a lower alcoholic and caloric count than regular wine. It was targeted primarily at women who are watching their calories or their alcohol intake. One of the most important research objectives was to gain some insight into how women perceived the attitudes of other people about them as a result of their drinking the product. The client was concerned that women drinking light wine would be viewed as prissy, or not "with it," which would have had significant implications on the advertising strategy if the wine were introduced.

The sentence completions that were used made it possible for the focus group moderator to get directly to the point. The participants were given a sheet of paper that contained the following partial sentences that they were asked to complete:

1. While I was in a local restaurant with a blind date, I ordered light wine before dinner. As soon as I placed the order with the waiter, my date must have felt _____

   _____

   _____

2. We were ordering drinks in the jazz bar, when my girlfriend ordered light wine. I felt that she _____

   _____

   _____

3. When my boyfriend ordered a light wine instead of a beer, I felt he _____

   _____

   _____

Each of these sentences elicited key information. The first sentence provided insight into how women thought men perceived them when drinking light wine. It raised discussions about whether it is fashionable or "nerdy" to drink light wine and what motivates people to drink light wine rather than the alternatives. The man in the scenario was identified as a blind date rather than a regular boyfriend so that the image projected would be an absolute—a blind date would have no basis for comparison—whereas a boyfriend probably would have compared the woman's behavior to something she had done before.

The second sentence elicited the participants' feelings about drinking the light wine in a "safe" environment. Since it is a friend who orders the wine, the participants could be as complimentary or critical as they wanted without criticizing themselves. In effect, they projected their feelings onto another woman, feelings that were likely to be what the participants themselves felt about the product.

The third sentence was a very easy way to find out the women's feelings toward male consumption of light wine. In the group discussion, it raised the question of whether light wine is a male or a female beverage, and it gave the moderator an excellent way to get the group to describe the type of man who would be likely to order this product.

Using Sentence Completions. To use sentence completions in a focus group, the following guidelines should be followed:

- The sentences must be short and very easy to understand, so the participants can write in their answers quickly.
- The sentences must be very specific, so that the information that the participants give falls into a very defined range.
- The participants must be given sufficient time to complete all the sentences before any discussion begins.

After all the sentences have been completed, the moderator should review the participants' responses to each sentence with the entire group, before proceeding to the next. The best way to do this is to ask each participant to read her response and to briefly explain it. Then the moderator should encourage the participants to respond to each other's reactions.

The moderator should proceed to the next sentence completion exercise only after the first one has been discussed in detail and no additional information of value can be obtained from further group interaction.

Sentence completions must be planned in advance to be effective, since the partial sentences must be carefully formulated. The sentence completion technique is not as flexible as forced associations, which can be incorporated into a focus group discussion at any time, whenever the moderator feels they will be helpful. On the other hand, sentence completions can generate input about a specific topic or question much better than the forced relationship technique can.

Expressive Drawing

Expressive drawing, another projective technique, can be very helpful in eliciting information that might otherwise not be generated in traditional focus group discussions. This technique can also energize a group when this becomes necessary. Some people refer to this technique as the Thematic Apperception Test (TAT), which is really just a fancy name for expressive drawing.

In expressive drawing, participants are asked to provide their reaction to a product or service by drawing a picture of how they feel about it. Each participant is usually given a small box of crayons and a blank piece of white paper to make their picture. They are given about three minutes to complete this task.

When all the drawings are completed, information can be elicited from the participants in two ways. The moderator can ask each person to show their picture and explain to the other participants what it means. The others are instructed to insure that the "artist's" drawing accurately reflects what *they* believe he or she is thinking by challenging the "artist," if necessary. The important part of this exercise is that each "artist" explains all aspects of the drawing and how it relates to the discussion topic.

The second way a moderator can use expressive drawing is to have the participants interpret each other's drawings, and the "artist" saying where the others are and are not correct. The advantage of this approach is that it involves the entire group of participants in developing interpretations of the drawings and hence of the product or source. The disadvantage is that it can prove time-consuming and wasteful if the people in the group have difficulty making their interpretations, and if the "artists" do not have the strength to say how they really feel even if it is not popular with the others. Also, some people become very inhibited when asked to provide a creative expression and are unable to provide anything useful for discussion purposes.

Anthropomorphization

In projective technique, information is generated by directing the participants to bring an inanimate object "to life." The moderator asks them each to write a brief story about the product or service, indicating what type of person it would be if it were a person. They are asked to give the product a human name, physical description, and series of likes and dislikes. Sometimes the participants are asked to indicate the type of relationship they would be likely to have with the anthropomorphized object.

By probing the participants about their stories, a well-trained moderator can often gain a great deal of insight into their feelings about the product or service and its perceived strengths and weaknesses. This is a very useful technique for gaining information about products or services that are difficult to talk about in traditional terms, such as toilet paper product, a ball bearing, or a mortgage service from a bank.

The main problem with anthropomorphization is that it can take a great deal of time that might be more productively used in other ways to get the same information.

Probing Techniques

Probing techniques, the second major class of new moderation techniques, are used by moderators to delve further into a specific discussion. The questioning methods and group exercises used differ from projective techniques in that they are less abstract and are normally easier to use with the average group. Probing techniques stimulate discussions about a specific topic that may not otherwise be possible.

Conceptual Mapping

In this very simple probing technique, a conceptual map is used to elicit information from participants. The participants are each given a conceptual map or asked to draw one on a blank piece of paper. The map looks like a tic-tac-toe game:

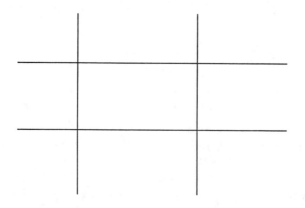

Suppose the research is being conducted to learn consumer attitudes about the image, strengths, and weaknesses of a particular foreign make of automobile, the Audi. The participants are asked to write down on the tic-tac-toe chart all the different brands of foreign automobiles that they can think of, grouping the ones that they see as similar in the same box. They can use as many boxes as they need, they are told, and should draw additional lines to create more boxes if necessary.

The participants are given about five minutes to complete the map. While they are working, the moderator draws a replica of the map on the easel, to be the vehicle for stimulating discussion.

When the writing time is over, the moderator should initiate the discussion by asking what categories the participants developed and their reasons for developing the ones they did. The objective here is to understand the group's thinking about the categories of foreign cars that they feel exist generally, not where they put the Audi. In fact, no mention of any specific car names is made at this point. Rather, the discussion aims to determine the rationale of the participants in creating the categories they created. Some participants may categorize foreign cars according to price, for example, and their conceptual maps will group cars in that manner. Other participants may classify foreign cars according to size, and still others according to perceived quality, which could lead to a discussion about how they decide what is a good car and what is not. Finally, some may classify according to their personal experiences, listing the foreign cars they have owned and identifying those they had good experiences with and those that were less than satisfactory. Needless to say, this provides many excellent opportunities for discussion.

There are probably many additional ways the group might categorize foreign cars, and the moderator should probe each participant to identify all the approaches and ensure that the participant has articulated why he or she arranged the cars this way.

In most conceptual mapping exercises, one predominant approach to classification emerges. This should become the focus of the discussion in the next part of the exercise. The moderator should reproduce its various segments on the easel by labeling the boxes in the matrix. Then the moderator asks the people who classified the cars this way to name the specific cars that they put into each box. This key part of the exercise will generate important information. First, the moderator will gain insight into the group's relative awareness about the various cars on the market. He or she should now find out how many participants put the Audi in any of the boxes on their sheet. The moderator should also ask how many put other major brands such as Mercedes and BMW in any of the boxes. This part of the exercise can indicate how broadly known the Audi is compared with other foreign cars.

The moderator should then have the participants discuss the cars in each category to get as much consensus as possible about where in the map each car make belongs. The moderator should then try to gain as much information as time permits about why people put the various products in the boxes that they did. Particular attention should be given to the box that contains the Audi.

The next focus of the discussion should be on determining why the Audi was placed in that box and not in another. The moderator should ask about the various cars that were put into the same box as the Audi: How similar to the Audi are they? This is an excellent opportunity to get in-depth comparisons with the Audi's competitors. The moderator might ask whether all the cars in the Audi's box are essentially the same. Normally, the group will say they are similar but there are some differences among them. The moderator can follow up by asking the group to focus in on the similarities and the differences between the Audi and the cars which were put into the same box.

The conceptual map discussion should continue as long as valuable information continues to be generated. The key is to gain input from all the participants, and to try to find areas of agreement and consensus as much as possible.

In using this device for many years, my experience is that it works very well in almost every situation. Occasionally, there is a product category in which the participants do not have sufficient awareness of the various competitors or in which real or even perceived differences among the available products are very few. In neither of these two situations does the conceptual mapping technique work well.

In summary, conceptual mapping is a "one-dimension" probing technique that draws on one variable: participants' *overall* sense of where different brands belong. The next probing technique is a two-dimensional methodology, for delving into areas that may evolve from a conceptual mapping discussion.

Attitudinal Scaling

Attitudinal scaling is also a mapping technique, but it is not used as frequently as conceptual mapping since it is not always appropriate to a session's subject matter. As a two-dimensional approach, it seeks to gain participant input into two different variables, or important characteristics, of a product—in contrast to conceptual mapping, which focuses on only one. Attitudinal scaling has participants identify the two most important attributes of a product or service, then determines how various brands are perceived relative to the trade-off between the two attributes. Suppose a focus group is being conducted to explore the attitudes of sinus sufferers toward a certain over-the-counter medication that counters the effects of sinus infections. All sinus medications vary widely in their effectiveness, and they also produce very different side effects. The ideal medication would be one that effectively dries up the sinuses and stops the headache pain associated with sinus infections, yet causes no negative side effects. But the reality is that all the brands appear to offer the consumer a trade-off between effectiveness and side effects.

The initial discussion concentrates on assessing the various characteristics of an effective sinus medication. The participants try to determine which are the most important characteristics of a sinus medication, such as:

- It clears the nasal passage.
- It stops headache pain.
- It stops a running nose.
- It clears the head.
- It reduces fever.

The group also discusses the negatives associated with various sinus medications, such as:

- It causes drowsiness.
- It eliminates the appetite.
- It can be habit forming.
- It cannot be used by people with certain medical conditions.

Then the participants are given a graphic (or are asked to reproduce it on a blank sheet of paper) like the one shown in the diagram:

They are asked to label the X and Y axes according to the two key criteria the research is seeking to measure, in this case putting "effectiveness" on one axis and "negative side effects" on the other. The upper end of the effectiveness measure is labeled "very effective" and the lower end, "not very effective." Similarly, the right-hand end of the side effects measure reads "many side effects" and the left end says "few side effects," as illustrated below:

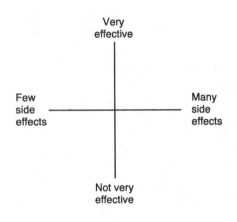

The participants are then asked to put the name of each brand of sinus medication of which they are aware—and of which they have a reasonable knowledge—on the place in the diagram that reflects their view of its relative effectiveness and side effects. The exercise forces the participants to think in general terms about sinus medications in a different way from normal thought patterns as they are forced to weigh their effectiveness against the side effects.

When the participants are finished, the moderator draws the scale on the easel. He or she then stimulates discussion by asking some of the participants to give their selections, which are placed on the grid in the appropriate places. The discussion focuses on trying to understand the differences in the participants' perceptions of the trade-offs between these variables. The moderator is likely to spend some time talking with the group about the various brands that compete with the client's product (as a way to disguise the purpose of the group), then focuses on the principal differences in the participants' reactions to the sinus medication that is being researched.

In summary, attitudinal scaling can be very helpful when the research objectives involve a trade-off between two variables that interact in a consumer decision. If handled properly, the technique can generate new thinking and insights about the entire product category and the key brands, since it requires the participants to think about these factors in a very different way than usual.

Laddering

Perhaps the most talked-about "new" tool in the focus group industry is laddering. Some moderators feel that it enables them to generate the same type of in-depth discussion as they would get in one-on-one interviews—but in a focus group. As a result, they feel that laddering offers the best of both worlds, both the positive aspects of group dynamics, and the multiple opinions available in focus groups, as well as the thoroughness of discussion indigenous to one-on-ones.

What Is Laddering? Laddering is a process in which the moderator probes the participants' innermost, underlying feelings behind a given issue. The essence of laddering theory is that the initial explanation that people give for a feeling they have is not the real explanation or the one that will make the difference in terms of reaching a target customer. Laddering, in theory, enables the moderator to get to the most personal, hidden reasons for why people feel they do about issues that on the surface do not seem particularly complex or even personal at all. It identifies the consumer "hot button" on a particular subject, enabling marketing communications to such individuals to be significantly more effective in the future than they have previously been.

The chart in Figure 7–3 shows a simplified version of a ladder that was developed in a focus group conducted to learn about consumers' real, inner feelings about eating a specific noncaloric food, which we will call Product M.

Implementation of Laddering. First, the moderator asks one of the participants for the principal reason they buy Product M. The participant likely responds that it is noncaloric. If the moderator feels this is probably not the principal reason why the person "feels" they

FIGURE 7-3
Laddering

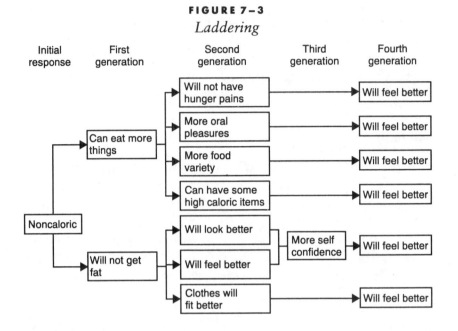

buy the product, he or she decides to use the laddering technique to try to find out why they "really" buy Product M.

The moderator goes on to ask why it is important that product be noncaloric. The participant's answer is likely to be either "you can eat more things" or "you will not get fat." Both represent logical answers to the question, but the moderator suspects that neither is the final answer. On the ladder, they become first-generation derivatives of the participant's initial response.

Suppose the participant's answer was "you will not get fat." The moderator then asks why not getting fat is particularly important to the participant. The participant is likely to respond that he or she "will look better," "will feel better," or that his or her "clothes will fit better." All three of these are certainly logical reasons why people do not want to get fat and why they might eat Product M. The answer becomes the second-generation derivative on the ladder. At this stage of the exercise, the moderator may decide to stop, since some personal reasons have been given that explain consumer purchasing behavior around the product. This could be the end of the ladder.

But some moderators will take this exercise further and try to gain even further explanations for participants' personal feelings and thereby find the "hot button" behind product positioning. They will take one of the second-generation answers and continue probing to see where it might lead. Suppose the participant had answered that they do not want to get fat so they will look better. The moderator will ask why it is so important to look better. One answer would be that the person "has more self-confidence" from looking better. For some moderators, this third derivative could be the end of the exercise.

The moderator may want to carry the ladder to its logical end, however getting to the final personal reason behind the person's decision to buy Product M. Probing the participant as to why having more self-confidence is important to them, the moderator is likely to get the response that the participant will "feel better." One could continue the ladder even further from here, or decide that this is a strong enough personal motivation to explain the reason for the purchase.

Use of Ladder Information. Ladder information is principally used from the creative perspective, in that the client now knows the most important personal reasons why people purchase Product M. Future advertising, promotion, and public relations focus on delivering the "feel better" message as a reason to purchase Product M. Communications should therefore be dramatically enhanced.

Commentary. As I mentioned at the beginning of this section, laddering is very much a "fad" technique in the early 1990s. And laddering certainly is an interesting and effective way to learn more about consumer motivations. But, it is my strong feeling that laddering is a much more appropriate tool for one-on-ones than for focus groups. Using laddering in focus groups, I feel does not do justice to the technique or to the focus group methodology.

For one thing, laddering requires that considerable time be taken with only one participant. It is very difficult to work a participant through a well-thought-out ladder exercise in less than ten or fifteen minutes. But this is simply too much time to allocate to one person in a focus group session. It tends to make the input of this individual seem disproportionately important to that of the other participants. Moreover, laddering forces the other nine participants to sit back and watch while the moderator goes through the exercise with the chosen person. This is boring for the others and precludes group input, even though it was to get group input that the focus group methodology was chosen in the first place. Finally, laddering is a very difficult technique to execute well, I believe, and it should be reserved for moderators who specialize in one-on-one research. It is an excellent research tool when used properly, but using it in focus groups eliminates much of its value. My recommendation is that laddering be used only in one-on-ones and not in focus groups.

Control Techniques

One of the most important advantages that focus groups have over other research techniques is the benefits that are obtained from people's interactions in groups—often referred to as group dynamics. Group dynamics are generally felt to be what distinguishes focus groups from other qualitative research techniques. Group dynamics is the process of securing information as an output or the interactions of several people in a group, as opposed to interviewing people individually. The group dynamics that occur when people interact about a topic stimulate the generation of more information than one might get from individual interviews. The synergy among the participants, the sum of their interactions in a group, is greater than the additive value individual interviews with each of them. An effective moderator can motivate the people in a session to communicate with each other as a way of exploring issues of common agreement or disagreement. This interaction generates a more complete picture of attitudes toward the subject than one would get from individual interviews.

The effectiveness of focus groups depends on the interactions among the participants. But these same interactions can (and frequently do) also impede the effectiveness of focus groups, under any of several circumstances. An opinion "leader" may emerge who influences the inputs of the other participants. As a result, the group discussion will reflect the opinion leader's views more than their own. (This can be particularly problematic in focus groups with young children.) In other cases, a very strong-willed person may intimidate some of the other participants, who subsequently say as little as possible for fear of alienating this person. Sometimes a few participants realize that they do not express themselves as well as the others and withdraw from the discussion for fear of looking stupid among the others. And finally, some participants feel a need to please the moderator and provide only positive feedback when asked for their opinions. Even when their feelings are not positive, they tend to give positive comments to please the moderator.

A number of techniques can be used to control the negative effects of group dynamics. They can be summarized as follows.

Assuring Participants' Authenticity

The best way a moderator can help the participants say what they really think and feel rather than be influenced by each other is to have them write down their opinions before they share them with the group.

Many different studies in social psychology suggest that people respond to stimuli differently when they write down their answer and when they share it aloud without first committing it to paper. If I held a turquoise-colored card up to a group of ten people, then asked each to tell me the color of the card, most people would be influenced by the inputs of those who spoke before them. If the first three people say the card is green, the others will likely follow suit— even if they really think it is blue. Further, the probability of that someone will contradict the group decreases dramatically as I ask the opinions of the last four people in a ten-person group. But if the participants are asked to write down the name of the color of the card before they speak, there is a significant probability that the tenth person will say it is blue if he thinks it is blue, even if everyone else before him said it was green. He might add a caveat, such as "the light is different where I'm sitting" or "I have very bad eyes," but at least we would get the individual's real opinion.

By applying this basic principle to focus groups, we can significantly eliminate the negative effects of group dynamics. During the course of an average focus group, I might ask the participants to write down their specific feelings or choices as many as seven times, often only a word or two, just to control the group dynamics. It works very well!

Controlling the Dominant Participants

It is not uncommon in focus groups for one participant to assume the role of group leader and try to dominate the session, either by talking excessively or by seeking to get the other participants to agree with his or her own view. There are several ways for a moderator to handle this type of situation:

Take Active Control. One technique is for the moderator to make sure that this individual knows who is in control of the group, and that the objective of the session is to hear from everyone about how they feel. The moderator can achieve this simply by taking active control of the group and indicating when people can and cannot talk. This might require the moderator to cut off the dominant person while he or she is "lecturing" the group, by calling on another person for their opinion. After the moderator does this a few times, the dominant personality will normally "get the message."

Enforced Silence. Another way to handle this situation is to ignore the dominant person whenever he or she tries to talk during the group. The moderator might pointedly omit calling on the person for his or her opinion and ask for the views of others. I find that after a half hour or so of this forced silence, a dominant person often gets the message and begins to function as an effective member of the group.

Explain the Problem. Another technique is for the moderator simply to explain to the dominant person that it is important for everyone in the group to participate and that their views must be heard as well. This is difficult to do without alienating the person and possibly others in the group, but it is sometimes the only alternative short of throwing him or her out of the group.

Remove the Participant. The last resort is for the moderator to throw the person out of the group. This should not be an option that a moderator uses very often. In the past ten years, I have had to do this only three times, and only when they proved uncontrollable. When someone gets into the group who cannot follow rules and insists on doing all the talking, each of the above techniques should be tried first, but sometimes the only recourse is removal. A moderator who decides on removal must follow a few simple rules, or he or she will risk alienating the entire group and thus dramatically reducing the probability that the session will achieve its objectives.

The first rule is to have a plan. The moderator should develop a signal with the observers behind the one-way mirror, so they know what is about to happen. When the moderator gives the signal, the observers are to go and get someone from the facility to take the person out of the room. This is normally done by telling the person they have a phone call. The person should be told to take their things with them when they leave the room. This approach prevents the other participants from knowing that it was the moderator who threw the person out of the group, since that could hurt the relationship between moderator and participants. The removal must look as if it were initiated by the facility; hence the telephone call guise.

If the remaining participants do catch on and ask why their fellow participant was removed, the moderator should explain that the person had difficulty participating as an effective group member and that each of the remaining people needed more time to participate. Giving this type of explanation is viewed as in the best interest of the remaining members, and it is normally well received.

Summary

Effective focus groups in the 1990s are run by moderators who use various tools and techniques to gain more information from the participants than one would normally get from straight conversation. The techniques described in this chapter are only a sampling of those used by the hundreds of moderators in the United States. But they are excellent examples of the major kinds of techniques. As moderators develop their own style, they create their own techniques to better achieve their clients' objectives.

New Techniques Outline

Projective Techniques
    Personality associations

      Variable
      Fixed
    Situational associations
    Forced relationships
    Sentence completions
    Expressive drawing
    Anthropomorphization
Probing Techniques
    Conceptual mapping
    Attitudinal scaling
    Laddering
Control Techniques
    Assuring participants' authenticity
    Controlling dominant participants

8

Litigation Focus Groups

One significant trend in the 1990s is the use of the focus group technique in the legal profession to help attorneys prepare for litigation. Focus groups are only just beginning to become popular with litigators and are limited to the very large cases, due to the costs and time required to use this methodology. This chapter briefly reviews the types of prelitigation focus groups being used today, why they are used, how they are executed, and what they typically cost. It also provides a series of suggestions to improve the overall effectiveness of focus groups in prelitigation preparation.

Why Litigators Use Focus Groups

Litigators use focus group research to prepare the most effective cases they can for their clients. The main kinds of information that attorneys are looking for in this research are:

- The issues that jurors are most likely to identify as the factors determining their verdict. This helps the attorneys decide how to best use their time in preparing for the trial, so that they can concentrate on developing arguments for those parts of the case that will have the most impact on the jurors' ultimate decision.
- How to present various arguments to the jurors so that they are sufficiently convincing to win the case. This includes the content of the arguments (that is, what material should be introduced to convince the jurors), the format (or how it is introduced), and the style in which the argument is made to the jurors.

- The impact that opposing arguments might have on the jurors. A defense attorney might try to identify the impact of the prosecuting attorney's argument on the jurors. This can help defense attorneys decide how to counter the prosecution's argument when they present their own arguments or cross-examine witnesses.

Techniques for Litigators

There are two principal approaches to using focus groups in litigation. They can be effectively used depending on the research objectives of the attorneys. This section discusses each technique, the research objectives for which it is typically used, how the sessions are conducted, and its strengths and limitations.

The Mock Trial

This approach is used to identify the key issues in a case and to provide insights to the attorneys that will help present their arguments so they will have the maximum possible impact on the jurors. This is the more comprehensive of the two approaches not only in the amount of information obtained but also in the time needed to implement it.

The mock trial is normally executed as follows. First, approximately twenty-five participants are recruited according to demographic, psychographic, and attitudinal criteria that resemble as closely as possible those of the jury that the attorneys feel will be ultimately selected.

The participants are normally needed for the bulk of a day at the research facility, so mock trial sessions are frequently conducted on weekends, when people are more often available for extended periods of time. (The participants are paid according to the amount of time that they spend at the facility.)

The participants are seated in a large room set up as a theater, then given three "presentations," each of which lasts approximately one hour. The three presenters are attorneys from the litigation firm; one represents the prosecutor, one the defense attorney, and the other the presiding judge. Typically, the prosecution attorney presents first, followed by a brief break and then the defense attorney's case. After hearing the defense case, the "judge" helps the "jurors" understand the legal issues in the case and the decisions they are asked to make.

At the conclusion of the judge's presentation the group is divided into two groups of twelve people, which are intended to represent two juries. These will determine the guilt or innocence of the defendant. Each jury elects its own foreman, then operates completely independently from the other group. They have no more contact with each other for the rest of the day.

The juries go into their rooms, where they have approximately one hour to decide on the merits of the case. This room is likely to be observable through a one-way mirror, so that the attorneys can get some appreciation for how the "jury" discusses the case.

At the end of the allotted hour, the jury makes a verdict and delivers it to the client. Joined by one or two lawyers from the client, a trained moderator leads a discussion with the jury about what the arguments were that led them to make the decision that they made. The discussion covers such topics as:

- The most important facts of the case, from the perspective of the jurors
- The most convincing arguments that both the prosecuting attorney and the defense attorney presented
- Areas of confusion that hindered some of the jurors in deciding on the innocence or guilt of the defendant
- The most significant problems the jurists had with either of the attorneys' presentations, especially elements that were not believable or that were easily refuted by the other attorneys

At the conclusion of these focus groups, the attorneys involved in the case should have an excellent understanding of what they need to do to develop the most effective arguments to win their case. Having two simultaneous "juries" operating gives all the research benefits of a larger sample and enables comparisons of the behaviors and attitudes of the two groups. This approach helps establish the most important issues in the case and identifies the most significant strengths and weaknesses of both the defense and prosecution arguments.

Issue-Oriented Approach

This approach uses a setup that is much more like that of a traditional focus group. The participants recruited, however, are also as similar as possible in demographics, psychographics, attitudes, and behavior to the real trial's potential jurors.

In this approach, a discussion is held between a moderator, an attorney adviser, and the "juror" participants, that lasts about two and a half hours. First, the "jurors" are presented with a synopsis of the case, including the most important facts that have led to the trial, and the principal arguments that the prosecuting and defense attorneys are expected to present. This presentation normally requires twenty minutes to a half hour and is generally made by one of the attorneys on the litigation team.

The jurors are then asked to write a brief summary for five to ten minutes. They are to indicate their understanding of what they believe are the most important points of the case and their views of the attorneys' presentations. Writing this down minimizes the negative effects of group dynamics, so that when they are asked to share their views with the group, they are not overly influenced by the views of others.

After the jurors are finished writing, the moderator leads the group in a discussion about the most important facts of the case and the effectiveness of the attorneys' arguments, from the jurors' point of view.

This issue-oriented approach is most useful after the mock trial approach has been used, when the attorneys have developed a better understanding about the most pivotal issues in the case. The attorneys may decide to vary the content of their argument from focus group to focus group until they find the one that is most effective with the "jurors." The mock trial approach gives less flexibility in trying out different arguments.

Maximizing the Effectiveness of Litigation Research

Focus group research can be a very effective aid for litigators in preparing for trials, as it can assist them in developing arguments that will increase their chances of success. Like other types of market research, however, it is important that focus groups be implemented properly. This section identifies several key considerations in planning and implementing focus groups for litigation.

Develop Specific Research Objectives before Deciding on the Methodology. These objectives should be agreed upon by all personnel within the last firm involved with the case, so that the methodology is consistent with them. They should be written down. The type of focus groups implemented will depend on the research objectives that have been established.

Pay Particular Attention to Participant Recruitment. It is essential that the characteristics of the prospective jurors be carefully defined and that the recruiting adhere to the predetermined criteria. It is also desirable if the "jurors" have not participated in focus group research before, as their knowledge of the process could be disruptive to the overall effort.

Rehearse the Presentations before They Are Actually Given to the Prospective Jurors. This ensures that the presentations are as polished as possible and will achieve the maximum communication and comprehension among the jurors. The quality of the "output" from the research is directly dependent on the quality of the inputs that the jurors receive. At the same time, it would be very wasteful to have to conclude at the end of the research that the prosecutor or the defense attorney "won" the case because of the quality of the presentation of the arguments rather than the effectiveness of the arguments themselves.

Ensure that the Presentations of the Prosecutor and the Defense Attorney are Made Equally Well. If one attorney is a much stronger personality and a more effective presenter than the other, he or she will affect the jurors for the wrong reasons. The output of the research is likely to be significantly affected, and the quality of the jurors' output relative to the content of the arguments will be minimized.

Use a Professional Moderator. The value of this research largely depends on how effectively the moderator can get the participants to share their real feelings about the facts of the case and whether the arguments were or were not convincing to them. The client should thoroughly brief the moderator in advance about the case, to ensure that the research objectives are understood. The client should permit the moderator to conduct the discussions with only minimal involvement from the attending attorneys. In fact, some of the most successful discussions are those that the client attorneys observe from behind a one-way mirror, avoiding becoming too involved with the participants.

Develop an Ongoing Working Relationship with a Trustworthy Moderator. Legal focus groups are more complex than those used for traditional market research. It is in the best interests of both the moderator and the legal client that each understand what is expected of the other and that they can work effectively together. The firm should "invest" in a qualified moderator by taking the time to develop a good working relationship with him or her. Variations in the specific techniques that work best for the firm should be explored and encouraged. This exploratory process, done over several different cases, will produce significant rewards when the techniques that evolve meet the needs of the client organization.

Costs of Litigation Research

The costs of litigation research depend on many of the same factors on which the costs of traditional focus groups depend. The following range of costs for some of the key elements are given in 1992 dollars.

Rental of Facility. The cost of renting a facility for a full day ranges from $1,250 to $2,000. The factors that account for this wide range include the location of the facility, the number of rooms needed, the length of time needed, and the time of day.

Recruitment. If twenty-six people are recruited for the research, a reasonable estimate of the recruiting charges is $2,250 to $3,000. The difference is in the specific recruiting criteria that are established for "qualified" participants.

Participant incentive. This is the honorarium that the participants are paid. The amount ranges from $50 to $200 per individual, depending on the amount of time they are required to be at the facility and the type of people they are. Typically, professionals, executives, and medical personnel are more expensive than housewives, blue-collar workers, and lower-level white-collar personnel.

Miscellaneous Facility Charges. Other potentially significant costs are charges for videotaping and food. The cost of food that is very basic (like a deli-type platter) range between $7.50 and $10.00 per individual. They can get much higher if more elaborate food is demanded.

Moderator Charges. The moderator's charges for developing the research process, creating the moderator guide, conducting the sessions, and developing a final report can be quite significant. They depend heavily on the experience of the individual moderator and on the amount of time that the client organization requires of him or her. Costs typically range between $3,000 and $5,500 for a one-day research session with a final report.

Summary

Litigation is a new area for qualitative research that is emerging in the 1990s. It is virtually impossible to determine how many law firms use focus group research, or how many sessions they conduct each year. But the relatively high cost of focus group research makes it appropriate only for very large cases whose outcome could involve significant dollars.

Over the next three to five years, focus group research will probably be used more frequently as law firms realize its value. As the technique grows in popularity, it will evolve into a different format, just as the traditional focus group methodology and approach has changed since it emerged as a commonly used research technique in the 1960s.

Litigation Outline

Why Litigators Use Focus Groups
Techniques for Litigators
   The Mock Trial
   The Issue-Oriented Approach

Maximizing the Effectiveness of Litigation Research
  Develop specific research objectives before deciding on the
    methodology
  Pay particular attention to participant recruitment
  Rehearse the presentations
  Make the prosecution and defense presentations equally well
  Use a professional moderator effectively
  Develop an ongoing relationship with a trustworthy moderator
Costs of Litigation Research
  Facility rental
  Recruitment
  Participant incentive
  Miscellaneous facility charges
  Moderator charges

9

Trends in the 1990s

Focus groups have been commonly used in market research since the late 1960s, although some packaged food marketing organizations used the technique as early as the late 1950s, and some people even trace the beginning of the focus group technique back to the publication in 1941 of *The Focused Interview* by Robert K. Merton, Marjorie Fiske, and Patricia Kendall. Most research practitioners agree, however, that the technique began to be used regularly only in the late 1960s and early 1970s and that it has grown in popularity every year since.

Like so many marketing devices, the more focus groups are used, the more they change, as professionals seek new ways to improve the technique. Indeed, the changes that have been made in the past twenty years in the United States are remarkable. As recently as 1973 I traveled to a small town on Long Island to conduct focus groups in someone's living room. In those days, it was common for a "facility" to be the den or living room in the home of someone from a local research company; the moderator and participants would discuss the research topic sitting on chairs and sofas. The client observers would listen from an adjacent room or sometimes even in the same room but off to the side. At that time, there were relatively few professional focus group facilities with specially designed focus group rooms, one-way mirrors, and audio and video recording capabilities.

In the 1970s participants were often recruited for focus groups from local churches, synagogues, civic or social groups. The client organization would make a donation to the sponsoring group for "borrowing" their people to talk about the topic of interest. The participants' "pay" would be the money their organization got for recruiting them. This scenario is quite different from that of today, when participants are recruited as *individuals* rather than groups— it has been determined that the best results from the research come when the participants do not know each other. Further, they themselves are paid to participate, rather than an organization.

In the 1970s, focus group moderating was not considered a subspecialty of market research, and it was not unusual for the moderating to be done by anyone at the client organization or agency who might be available, from the agency president to the account executive—even a secretary from the research department. There were very few specialists in qualitative research, and virtually nobody made a living conducting focus groups. Contrast this with 1991, when the best industry estimates indicate that 800 to 1,000 people earn the bulk of their livelihood conducting focus groups, and the average full-time moderator conducts almost a hundred groups per year.

In the 1970s, the typical advance preparation for a focus group consisted of a very brief discussion between the client and the researcher, often just before the participants arrived. The researcher would develop a very brief outline of material to be covered during the session, often amounting to only a few notes to serve as a reminder of the client's requirements for the session. This is quite different from the situation today, when most moderators allocate considerable time to developing a guide, thinking through the subject matter, and deciding on the most effective techniques to elicit information from the participants.

In 1970, it was normal procedure to record the discussion with a tape recorder placed in the middle of the living room or on the dining-room table. The moderator would be responsible for watching the machine so that the tape could be changed every thirty or sixty minutes, as needed. At that time, there was little expectation that focus groups would soon be conducted in soundproof rooms with highly sophisticated equipment recording the action for immediate playback the next day.

In the 1970s, it was not unusual for an individual focus group participant to attend dozens of sessions each year, recruited by their community organizations. Few people in those days understood the problem of the "professional respondent," let alone that one day computerized services would be used to identify people who attend too many groups.

These are some of the most obvious changes that have occurred in the focus group industry in the past twenty years. They highlight the maturing that this business has undergone in almost all aspects of the focus group process. The significant changes of the past twenty years can only lead us to assume that innovation will continue, and that many more important changes will occur in the 1990s.

This chapter outlines some of the changes that I anticipate will be made in focus groups over the next decade. These changes involve eight basic areas of the focus group process:

- volume
- the moderator
- implementation
- facilities
- moderation techniques
- the role of the client
- costs
- technology

A logical question the reader might ask at this point is whether it is relevent to speculate about changes that might occur in the industry in the next few years. I feel it is vital not only for an overall understanding of focus group methodology at present but as an aid to persons considering a career in focus groups into the twenty-first century. A person with a reasonable understanding of both the history and the future of the focus group methodology will be in a much better position to evaluate the desirability of a career in focus groups as a moderator, a qualitative researcher, or a facility staffer.

My predictions about the major trends that we will see in the business over the next few years are as follows.

Increased Volume

The number of focus groups conducted will increase significantly. Leading research industry groups estimate that approximately 110,000 focus group were conducted in the United States in 1990. Although the number has been increasing very quickly in recent years, there is no official industry data on the rate of the increase. Still, a key question for anyone considering a career in focus groups is where they are going in the next ten years: Will the volume remain essentially the same, or will it increase significantly?

In my opinion, it would not be surprising to see 200,000 focus groups conducted each year by the late 1990s—almost double the number at the present time. The reasons for this anticipated increase in volume are several.

First, organizations that have only "dabbled" in the focus group arena up until now will use them more frequently. Corporations, nonprofits, law firms, educational, and governmental institutions will place more value on the use of qualitative research in their planning and assessment processes. New persons coming to these organizations who have successfully used focus groups in the past will stimulate interest in them in their new organizations.

Second, I believe that the market research industry will tend to shift from quantitative to qualitative research, making more money available for focus groups. This phenomenon will occur for three principal reasons:

- Profit pressures will require companies to reduce their research budgets, and qualitative studies are generally considerably less expensive than quantitative studies. They will shift from quantitative to qualitative research, using a series of four to six groups (which will cost about half), recognizing that the information generated is less precise but still valuable.

- Senior management will encourage middle-level managers to use qualitative research as an input into the decision making process, along with their experience and judgment. In essence, senior management will tell their managers to earn their "big salaries" by using less expensive research vehicles and more judgment based on their experience.

- There will likely be a consumer backlash against telephone and mall intercept research studies, as people become more protective of their privacy. The cost of telephone and mall intercept research will consequently increase to such a degree that it will only be used when absolutely necessary. Qualitative research will be employed instead, as it requires fewer contacts to complete a study.

- The quality of the focus group "product" will increase significantly in the future, as more professionals enter the field on both the client and the service-provider ends. Overall standards of focus group research will rise as moderators invent new techniques, clients demand more professionalism, and facilities significantly upgrade the quality of their recruiting and the physical plant.

The Moderator

The typical moderator of the 1990s will be a person whose background is in line marketing and/or sales, rather than market research, psychology, or sociology. The reason for this is that clients will expect moderators to bring significantly more "added value" to the research process than they do now, being able to provide insights about the action-oriented marketing or the sales implications of the research findings. No longer will moderators be qualified simply because they can moderate groups effectively and write good final reports. If they cannot turn the research results into specific recommendations, they will not be able to compete.

Moderator as Partner

The moderator of the 1990s also will be viewed as a *partner* in the overall marketing effort of the client organization, not simply a *vendor* of research services. He or she will be viewed as a professional, much as corporations consider the lawyers and accountants with whom they work regularly. Moderators will offer a much higher level of professional services than they did in the past, and they will be selected based on their potential overall contribution to a project rather than on the low level of the bid that they submit.

Professional Certification

The research industry will also attempt to institute professional certification requirements for focus group moderators, perhaps like a CFP (certified financial planner) or a CPA (certified public accountant). Requiring moderators to meet certain standards in order to carry the "seal of approval" of the accrediting body would be an important step toward giving qualitative research the professional status it deserves. This process will probably begin in the mid-1990s but will probably not be completed for several years. This area is currently being evaluated by the QRCA (Qualitative Research Consultants Association) and probably will become a reality in the next few years as more new people enter the industry.

Implementation

The 1990s will see many changes in the implementation of focus group research. These will include the following.

Schedule Changes

Daytime will become a more popular time to conduct focus group sessions, since it is becoming increasingly difficult to motivate people to come for evening groups, particularly those at eight o'clock. Early morning sessions (held at around seven-thirty) will become very popular, particularly for business and professional groups. More focus groups will also be conducted over the noon hour, to take advantage of the availability of working personnel during their lunch hour. Finally, more focus groups will be conducted on weekends, due to the greater availability of working people to participate at that time.

Shortened Length

Focus groups will also tend to be shortened to one and one half hours (from the current two), in order to be able to finish groups held in the early morning and noontime hours. Shorter-length groups will also become popular in the evening, in order to end the sessions earlier—at nine or nine-thirty rather than ten o'clock—since the quality of the information generated often disintegrates as the hour draws later.

More Minigroups

More minigroups (six participants) will be used instead of full groups (ten people), in order to keep the costs of focus groups as low as possible. Moreover, it will be increasingly difficult to recruit focus group participants, so smaller groups will become more acceptable.

Moderator-Observer Communication

Communication between the moderator and the client observers in the back room will also change significantly. Today, many moderators and their clients interact by means of notes sent to the moderator from the back room. As researchers become more sophisticated and more sensitive to the dynamics of moderator-participant interaction, note-passing will be used less and less. Rather, moderators will build into the guide opportunity times to go into the back room to communicate directly with the observers. They will do this in various ways that do not have a negative effect on group dynamics (as note-passing does) yet that at the same time will permit the moderator time to interact with the client observers while the group is in session.

Better Facilities

Focus group facilities and the services they provide will also undergo significant changes.

Physical Plant

The physical plant of facilities will get better and better as new companies enter the field and new facilities are built. Focus group rooms will be larger (to avoid the cramped feeling in many facilities now), back-room observation areas will be more comfortable, and the one-way mirrors will be larger and provide greater visibility. The newer facilities will provide one-way viewing from at least two different directions, so that the observers can move around and thereby feel more in contact with the group participants.

Integrated Services

The focus group facility of the 1990s will be more of a full-service supplier than those of today. They will offer full moderation and analysis capabilities, not just a place to hold the sessions. Vertically integrating their services will mean excellent incremental profit opportunities for facilities while better meeting the needs of their clientele.

Videotaping

Videotaping with a fixed camera will be established as a regular part of the focus group fee rather than an extra cost. When a camera operator is needed to make a higher quality tape, additional costs will be incurred. But most facilities will incorporate a fixed videocamera into their room design and automatically tape the groups for their clients.

In-house Recruiting

Facilities will do more of their own recruiting, rather than contract it out to others who do it on a part-time basis from their homes. This will be brought about by clients' demands for more control over the recruiting of participants, in view of increasingly tighter screening criteria.

Moderating Techniques

The 1990s will also see some important changes in moderation techniques. The typical focus group will be more than a ninety-minute discussion between moderator and participants. Greater demands will be placed on moderators to conduct groups that more effectively generate the information clients need.

Moderator Guides

Moderator guides will become a much more important part of the process than they are now. Each element of the session will be analyzed in great detail by both client and moderator before it even begins. Guides will receive the same degree of attention from client research and marketing personnel that quantitative questionnaires receive now.

Emphasis on Interaction

Much greater emphasis will be placed on encouraging interaction among group participants. Many moderators now conduct sessions as if they were ten separate one-on-one interviews, with the bulk of the discussion occurring directly between them and individual participants. In the future, clients will demand significantly more interaction among the participants, so that group dynamics can be used to elicit various points of view from the participants.

External Stimuli

The use of external stimuli to elicit responses from participants will become more widespread. Researchers will recognize that focus group research works best when the participants become involved with the subject matter and are asked to react to specific things. New projective techniques will be developed to help moderators probe participants' attitudes toward different topics. Other types of stimuli will be created and used in which individuals express their feelings by responding to something or doing something (like drawing or rearranging elements) rather than by articulating their feelings verbally.

Expanded Role of the Client

Clients will become much more involved in the focus group process than they have been in the past.

The Briefing

Briefing the moderator will become the responsibility of the marketing department rather than the research department. This will be in recognition of the importance of providing the right information to the moderator, so that he or she will know what nuances to listen for as the discussion unfolds.

Moderator Guide

The moderator guide will be reviewed in depth by the marketing people as well as market research, to ensure that the correct material will be covered during the group and that appropriate time is allocated to each topic.

Client Observers

More people from client organizations will attend focus groups in the future than do at present. Project leaders will seek to involve as many people from their company as possible who can be helpful to the project's overall success. It will not be unusual for people representing engineering, production, sales, and research and development to observe groups, in addition to the marketing and strategic planning people who are traditionally involved.

Increased Costs

The 1990s will see significant increases in the cost of focus groups. If the average cost of a focus group was $3,400 in 1990 (as estimated by the Advertising Research Foundation), the price of a group may reach as high as $8,000 by the year 2000, representing approximately a 9 percent annual compounded increase. The costs may rise because new facilities will be built with more amenities and a better physical plant, and costs of these improvements will ultimately have to be borne by the end user. Other cost factors at the facility end of the business will also add to focus group costs, such as "free" videotaping and in-house recruiting.

Still another factor will be greater fees charges by moderators. As the research industry demands more professional moderators who can provide meaningful "added value" to sessions, the cost of their time will increase. The time involved in planning and analyzing focus group sessions will rise in the 1990s as clients demand better moderator guides, external stimuli, and final reports. Moderator charges are normally directly related to the amount of time needed to complete these.

Use of Technology

The 1990s will see the following trends emerging in the technology associated with focus groups.

Personal Computers

The use of the personal computer to stimulate discussion during sessions will increase. Because of the greater capabilities and user-friendliness of computer graphics, and the advent of computer-aided design programs, participants will be increasingly exposed to concepts, designs, and new product ideas through computer images. Response to these images during the group discussion will be used to modify the visual as the session progresses to reflect the participants' inputs. Artists in the back room will draw new concept sketches based on the comments from the people in six o'clock groups, to be exposed to the next group at eight o'clock.

Remote Broadcasts

The proceedings of focus groups will be broadcast live to the offices of clients who cannot or will not travel to the locale where the group is being conducted. This technology is presently being offered in a few locations in major markets, but it will become much more broadly available in the next few years. It will be available at an extra cost to all clients but not all clients will wish to utilize it. The key people in client organizations will get much more out of focus groups if they can experience the proceedings firsthand, without distractions, and they will also have the ability to interact personally with the moderator during the group and between sessions from remote locations.

Satellite Videotransmissions

Satellite video transmissions will become an integral part of the focus group industry. Much as corporations currently use videoconferencing to enable people in remote locations to meet with others in different locations, some focus groups will also leverage this technology. Focus groups will be implemented with half the group located in one city with the moderator and the other half in another city with a co-moderator or assistant. Using videoconferencing, clients will be able to secure inputs from and interact with two groups in very distant geographic areas. In the 1990s, when global marketing will become a household word, global focus groups via video-conferencing will fit the research needs of the market very well.

Telephone Groups

The 1990s will also see even less use of the telephone focus group, as researchers recognize the weakness of the technique and use other methodologies to accomplish the same objectives.

Screening Clearinghouses

Massive clearinghouses will be used to assist in the screening process, so that facilities can be sure that participants are not "professional respondents" working in several different facilities in the same area. At present, screening questionnaires generally are used to try to identify (and then terminate) people who have recently participated in other groups (within the previous three to six months); but accuracy depends on respondents honestly answering the questionnaires. In the 1990s a facility will be able to enter the person's name and telephone number into a database to determine their previous participation.

Summary

The focus group industry will probably experience more changes during the 1990s alone than were realized in the past thirty years. The popularity of the technique will cause a great incentive both in the research community and in the client universe to make it as effective as possible. There will be greater pressure on moderators to develop their competitive advantages and on facilities to offer the very best. Dramatic improvements in all parts of the industry will generate important benefits to clients and will increase the moderators' and facilities' professionalism.

Trends in the 1990s Outline

Increased Volume
The Moderator

Moderator as partner
Professional certification
Implementation
Schedule changes
Shortened length
More minigroups
Moderator-observer communication
Facilities
Improved physical plant
Integrated services
Videotaping
In-house recruiting
Moderation Techniques
Moderator guides
Emphasis on interaction
External stimuli
Expanded Role of the Client
The briefing
The moderator guide
Client observers
Increased Costs
Use of Technology
Personal computers
Remote broadcast
Satellite videotransmissions
Fewer telephone groups
Screening clearinghouses

Threats to the Focus Group Industry

Most people who have been involved in market research over the past fifteen years would likely agree that the unprecedented growth in the use of focus groups has been the most significant industry trend during this period. Unfortunately, there are no official industry statistics that quantitatively measure the number of focus groups conducted each year, but it is not unrealistic to estimate that the number of sessions conducted in 1992 will be more than double that of 1982—only ten years earlier.

Will this trend continue? In Chapter 9, predictions were made about everything from changes in the methodology to costs. But there are factors that threaten the focus group industry. Major industry associations such as the Qualitative Research Consultants Association (QRCA), the Market Research Association (MRA), the Advertising Research Foundation (ARF), and the Council of American Survey Research Organizations (CASRO) can take steps to counter these threats. This chapter examines the key threats to the industry and what these associations might do to minimize their potentially negative impact on the industry.

Threats to the Industry

Recruitment Abuses

The most significant threat to the focus group industry is recruitment abuses, in which the wrong people are recruited for sessions. These abuses result from several different phenomena.

Recruitment Scams. Recruitment scams are perpetrated by organizations that tell potential participants they can "make money fast" by essentially becoming "professional respondents" in focus groups. They generally work as follows.

An entrepreneur advertises easy money for participation in market research, in newspapers or on retail store bulletin boards. Prospects are told to call an 800 telephone number or write to an address to get a "kit" that will enable them to make money on research. The kit costs anywhere from $49 to $99 (according to what we know about these scams so far). The "kit" normally contains a list of names and addresses of all market research facilities in the area, and an instruction "manual" that tells candidates how to contact the facilities in order to become one of their subjects. They are instructed not to tell the facility how they got its name and number or what motivated their call. The material also advises the candidate what not to say when questioned by a facility, so that they will be sure to qualify for participation in research.

The problem with these organizations is that if they become successful, it will be very difficult to conduct focus groups with "fresh" respondents who have not previously participated in many sessions and who are not participating solely to make money. The shortage of really qualified participants will mean reduced confidence in the focus group technique.

What Can Be Done to Minimize This Problem? It is almost impossible to completely eliminate organized scams, but there are several things that the industry can do to minimize their impact.

- Trade groups can try to stop these organizations from operating by using whatever legal means might be possible. Industry groups are likely to obtain better professional legal counsel than individuals operating such sleazy businesses can. It is hoped that each venture can be stopped by legal tactics shortly after it is discovered.
- Focus group facilities must be alerted to these scams and not accept participants for their internal databases unless the facility has contacted them, rather than the other way around. This will require facilities to take a more proactive approach in developing their recruitment lists, but it is vital for protecting their own future in qualitative research.

- Clients and moderators can insist that their facilities recruit only from telephone books or purchased lists. This will preclude the use of databases—the mainstay of facility recruiting efforts at present. This will raise the cost of focus groups by 20 percent or even more, but it will maintain the integrity of the recruiting effort and will result in more qualified participants.

Facility Cheating. Some facilities and independent recruiters try to increase the profitability of their recruitment activities by cheating in several ways.

- Accepting respondents for their databases based on incoming telephone calls—perpetuating the problem of recruitment scams.
- Prompting candidates to participate in a prospective group that will tell them how to conform to screening criteria. For example, if a facility is seeking people who have eaten a particular food in the past six months, it could ask them to purchase the product beforehand to ensure that they qualify for the upcoming session.
- Leveraging "qualified" respondents to find others. If the facility is seeking people who belong to a duplicate bridge club, for example, it might ask accepted candidates for the names of people they know who belong to such clubs.
- Telling candidates to lie about certain recruitment criteria so that they qualify for the group, such as their income level, their frequency of purchasing a specific product, or their awareness of a certain product.

What Can Be Done to Minimize This Problem? Unlike recruitment scams, facility cheating is a very difficult problem to correct, since the organizations fostering the abuse would normally be the ones to stop it. Further, there is a short-term financial incentive for facilities to cheat. Still, there are a few actions that the research industry can take to reduce the incidence of these activities.

- Implement an education program aimed at facilities and other recruitment organizations to inform them of the long-term danger to their business of recruitment abuses. If they understand that the financial benefits from these activities are very short term, it is hoped that they will eliminate them for the long-term good of their business.

- Enlist moderators to be hypersensitive to the recruitment abuses and to watch for possible abuses during the course of the groups. A moderator who determines that a facility has cheated in its recruiting should bring this to the attention of the owner, demanding a full explanation. If the response is not sufficient, the moderator should refuse to pay the facility for its "services."
- Implement an industrywide program of information-sharing about recruitment services, in which moderators share both good and bad experiences. At present, the QRCA has initially attempted this by publishing a "city list," but such efforts must go much further if they are to significantly protect the industry.
- Develop peer-review groups and industry trade associations to monitor recruitment activities. In my opinion, this is by far the best way to correct the problem, as the vast majority of focus group facilities in the United States are very professional and are extremely upset about the abuses of others. If the good facilities can band together to raise industry standards, the entire industry will benefit.

Inappropriate Cost Increases

Another major threat to the focus group industry is the increasing cost of this type of research. At present focus groups are a reasonably efficient qualitative research method. But from the perspective of cost per interview (that is, the total cost of the group divided by the number of people in it), focus groups are dramatically more expensive than quantitative research.

As focus groups continue to increase in popularity, the demand for qualified moderators and excellent facilities may exceed the supply. The net effect of this could be that moderators and facilities become greedy and opportunistic, raising prices beyond what is considered reasonable. If this happens, the cost-value ratio of focus groups could become unfavorable compared with other research methods. The ultimate impact would be a reduced demand for focus groups.

What Can Be Done to Minimize This Problem? While it will be impossible to eliminate some cost increases, the rate of the increases should be controlled so that they are consistent with overall economic conditions. This objective can be achieved in two ways:

- Industry trade associations should monitor the cost of focus groups and publish articles in key journals identifying cost trends. These articles should seek to educate the various parties to the process about the impact that their cost increases will have on the future use of the focus group technique.
- Client organizations should use their influence to control anticipated cost increases. While the cost of focus groups can be expected to increase somewhat over time, the amount of the increases should be carefully monitored by the market research departments of client organizations. When they are presented with charges that appear to be out of line with industry norms, they should refuse to accept the proposed charges. They should require the service provider to justify the costs on an item-by-item basis, considering recruitment costs, facility expenses, and moderator charges separately.

Lower Level of Moderators' Professionalism

A potential by-product of the growth of the focus group industry is the influx of inexperienced or unqualified moderators into the business. Because the industry is currently not regulated, anybody can claim to be a focus group moderator. Further, virtually no financial investment is needed to become a moderator, and on the surface the profession does not appear to require much technical knowledge, so it seems to be a very attractive career option for people who are unhappy in their present jobs or who wish to start their own business.

The problem with this influx of inexperienced people is that the overall quality of moderators' work will almost certainly be reduced. As moderators learn the business at the expense of their clients, the result could be client dissatisfaction and even a disenchantment with the focus group technique itself because "it doesn't work." Predictably, this will reduce the use of the technique in favor of other qualitative or quantitative techniques.

What Can Be Done to Minimize This Problem? The market research industry can minimize this problem in several ways.

- Industry associations like the QRCA, AMA, and ARF should work together to develop an accreditation process for new people entering the field. While this would be very difficult to do, requiring new moderators to undergo certification would give a degree of professionalism to experienced moderators and protect standards of professionalism among moderators generally.
- Active practitioners can write articles for relevant marketing and market research publications and give speeches to appropriate audiences about the importance of the moderator in focus groups. The will help raise consciousness among the users of qualitative research, so that they will be more selective about the moderators they retain.
- Moderators themselves can make training positions available in their practices, so that new moderators have a viable way to learn the profession. These training positions would be not unlike the internships that physicians, psychologists, architects, and engineers must often take before they go off on their own. For this approach to work, however, the industry must recognize that these internships are training positions, which places a great responsibility on the trainers to see that their interns are effective. It would require close supervision on the part of the trainers.
- The users of focus group research must be willing to demand either experienced moderators or interns supervised by qualified moderators, even though they will be more expensive than inexperienced, unsupervised moderators.

General Disenchantment

Market research methodologies, like many elements of marketing, go through cycles of popularity. In the 1960s, for example, motivational research was a very popular technique. Today you would be hard pressed to find anyone conducting motivational research, and most of the younger people entering the industry have likely not even heard of it.

In the 1970s, simulated test marketing was a very popular quantitative technique that combined consumer attitudes and behavior with marketing and sales inputs to predict the market share that a new product would achieve if introduced. The technique produced a long litany of success stories—as well as many less-than-accurate predictions. Today some research companies still aggressively promote prediction models, but this technique's popularity is only a fraction of what it was just a few years ago.

The reader may think that this could not happen to focus groups, since they are presently such a mainstay of market research and enjoy such wide popularity across virtually all industries and in both large and small companies. The technique may seem too "hot" at the moment to ever join the list of forgotten market research methods. But it is my strong opinion that the future of the focus group technique is entirely in the hands of the people who presently make their living by doing it. If practitioners become complacent because the demand is strong and they do not have to work hard to get new clients, the popularity of focus groups will probably decline over the next decade. On the other hand, if practitioners recognize that all products and services to through a life cycle, and that these cycles must be managed, then the future of focus groups is very positive.

How the Industry Can Counter These Threats

It is definitely within the control of the practitioners to control the destiny of the focus group technique. Actions that can be taken to achieve this objective include the following.

Seek Innovation

All focus group moderators must seek innovative techniques in conducting groups that will improve the quality of the inputs generated. This innovation should be comprehensive, considering at least the following areas:

- Developing more effective moderator guides that eliminate the "nice to know" information and focus on the topics necessary to achieve the research objectives
- Identifying more effective external stimuli so that concept

statements, product prototypes, and advertising or
promotion concept examples are more effective in generating
meaningful inputs from groups
- Developing better approaches to moderating that maximize
the positive effects of group dynamics and minimize the
negative effects
- Producing better final reports that are more action oriented
and more useful for client organizations

Openness and Sharing

Moderators must be more willing to share the techniques they use
with others. Traditionally, moderators have been quite secretive
about their techniques in order to maintain a competitive advantage
over other moderators. But if the industry is to move forward and if
focus groups are to continue to meet the needs of clients, it will be
necessary for moderators to share information to raise the general
quality of the research. In effect, each practitioner will have to view
himself or herself as an ambassador of the technique, with the mission
of raising the quality of the work conducted in the entire industry.

Industry Threats Outline

Threats to the Industry
   Recruitment abuses
      Recruitment scams
      Facility cheating
   Inappropriate cost increases
   Lower level of moderators' professionalism
   General disenchantment
How the Industry Can Counter These Threats
   Seek innovation
   Openness and sharing

11

A Career as a Moderator

This chapter is intended to help you decide whether a career as a focus group moderator is a good choice for you in the light of your career and lifestyle objectives. It discusses the options available to you if you do seek training as a moderator, and it suggests the activities you must undertake to build a moderation business.

Types of Moderators

At present there are approximately one thousand people who make most or all of their livelihood conducting focus groups. This is only an estimate, since there is no official trade group to whom all participating moderators must report, and even the largest industry associations (the QRCA, AMA, and ARF) have only a relatively small percentage of all moderators in their membership. Further, there are many part-time moderators who would like to earn their entire living in this profession but have not yet succeeded in doing so.

There are several different types of moderators of focus groups.

Self-Employed Full-Time Moderators. These moderators earn virtually one hundred percent of their income by moderating focus groups. They work full time at this task, normally on their own except for support staff like a secretary and a field coordinator. The average moderator conducts one hundred or more focus groups per year, as well as some one-on-ones and dyads. Some moderators also work as meeting facilitators, as leaders of creative idea generation sessions such as synectics, or in other roles relating to directing group discussions.

Self-Employed Part-Time Moderators. These moderators conduct focus groups as a part-time activity while they do other work such as marketing consulting, teaching, psychological counseling, freelance editing, and the like.

Employees of Market Research Companies. A large percentage of the moderators in the United States work for market research companies whose principal service is custom research. They are company employees and normally rely on the company to source clients for them and to provide the administrative, marketing, and technical support needed for their groups. This is the entry-level position in the focus group field for many moderators, as they develop their skills and clientele while working for the company, then leave to establish a practice for themselves.

Employees of Nonresearch Companies. Many corporations have their own market research departments, employing people to conduct focus group research for the organization. Many companies contract out the quantitative research they need to independent research organizations but implement focus groups in-house, using their own employees as the moderators. They feel that this saves them money, gives them more control over quality and timing, and produces more effective focus groups. These in-house people often function as internal consultants, viewing the "line" people in the company (with the research budget) as their clients and providing for them the same level of service that they would expect from an outside supplier.

Employees of Advertising or Public Relations Agencies. Advertising and public relations agencies are relatively heavy users of qualitative research, and many of them retain in-house personnel to handle this function for them. A large percentage of the qualitative research they perform is to help in developing new business, which is not billable. Many organizations therefore operate their own departments to save money on research.

People Between Jobs. Other moderators are people who have been terminated or laid off from marketing or research positions (due to their job performance *or* to economic conditions) and need to generate income until they find a new job. They are a very common phenomenon in the 1989–1992 period, as corporations cut back their staffs to reduce expenses. Many of these people view moderating as only a temporary, interim job rather than a career.

Advantages and Disadvantages

It is important for you to understand the advantages and disadvantages of focus group moderating in order to determine if it is the type of profession to which you want to dedicate your life. This section outlines what I believe are the most important advantages and the most significant limitations of a career as a moderator. This discussion is limited to moderating, which is very different from the business of operating a focus group research facility in terms of financial requirements, potential rewards, and business development. (Career opportunities in facilities are discussed in *The Practical Handbook and Guide to Focus Group Research*.)

Advantages

A career moderating focus groups offers some very important benefits.

Independence. As a focus group moderator, you can operate as an independent business person relatively easily, having excellent control over your own life and time. If you choose not to work on Wednesdays, for example, you can schedule your groups for other days of the week. Similarly, if you plan a vacation, you simply indicate to clients that you are not available for groups between certain dates. Further, you are accountable to nobody but your clients for the amount of work you do, the quality of your work, and the revenues you generate.

Self-Dependence. A major benefit of a moderating career for some people is that their overall performance depends almost exclusively on how well *they* have done *their* job. If the field service effectively recruits participants (an assumption that is not always warranted, as discussed in detail in Chapter 10), the relative success of a focus group research project will depend on how well the moderator prepares for the session, moderates the group, and presents the final report to the client. For people who have difficulty relying on others or who are not satisfied with the performance they normally get from other people, moderating can be an excellent career, since the moderator is primarily responsible for a project's success or failure.

Ease of Entry. Unlike many other professions, focus group moderation is one career where you do not have to get a license or even go through an accreditation process to practice. If you want to be a moderator, you can simply declare yourself available and "hang out a shingle." You have only to understand the focus group process and be able to convince client organizations to pay you to implement them.

Low Cost of Entry. Few careers can be started with a lower cost of entry than that of a focus group moderator. With only a telephone and a word processor, you can open an "office" as a moderator. There are no essential capital requirements and no inventory to purchase. You do not even need employees in your business, as long as you have a sufficiently low volume of groups to do your own scheduling, field coordination, and report production. Once you become busy, you will need employees to coordinate with field services to set up the groups for you, and secretarial support to develop your reports.

Intellectual Challenge. A career as a moderator is perfect for an individual who seeks intellectual stimulation on a regular basis. Moderators must become reasonably familiar with a large number of different types of businesses, in order to be able to develop effective moderator guides and ask the right questions during focus groups. Doing this type of preparation frequently involves significant advance planning, thinking, and studying, often involving material that is completely new to you.

Variety. Few careers offer the variety that moderating focus groups provides. It is not unusual for moderators to work in eight or ten completely different types of businesses within one month, each of which is dealing with completely different issues. In a four-week period, not only will you work in several different industries but you might work on customer service in one, new product concept development in another, packaging in a third, advertising assessment in a fourth, and so on. As a result, you never hear focus group moderators complain that their work is boring, since it is always changing and each project is generally quite different from the one that preceded it.

Professionalism. Most organizations regard focus groups as a specialty area of marketing, and moderators are therefore generally thought of as professionals in their field. This gives you a certain degree of prestige among clients, as moderators are generally considered to be "gurus" when it comes to designing and implementing focus group research. Therefore, it you are interested in having a profession within the marketing industry, focus group moderating is a very good area to consider.

Financial Rewards. Last but clearly not least, a career moderating focus groups can be very lucrative for people who can develop a clientele for it. It is not uncommon for a moderator to earn in excess of $150,000 per year, and many make substantially more than that if they have developed a large, active clientele.

Disadvantages

Although the benefits of a career as a moderator may make it seem like an extremely appealing profession, some aspects of the work are sufficiently negative that many people choose not to enter the field. Others work as moderators for only a few months or years. The most significant drawbacks are as follows.

Extensive Travel. Most moderators are required to travel regularly to conduct focus groups in various parts of the country (or world), to meet with clients to prepare for the session, and to present the results of the research. It is not unusual for a moderator to be traveling 50 percent or more of the time.

Night Work. The vast majority of focus groups are conducted in the evening, usually at six and eight o'clock. Focus groups held during the day probably account for fewer than 20 percent of all groups held. Therefore, if you embark on a career as a moderator, you must resign yourself to spending most of your working time after "normal" working hours.

Competitiveness. The focus group research industry is extremely competitive: a large number of moderators are competing for business. Even worse, it is very difficult for a moderator to articulate a meaningful "reason why" a client should use him or her rather than another moderator. It is difficult to develop a regular clientele in the qualitative research business, and many moderators find that the only way they can successfully compete is to offer their services at lower than "market" rates. This can result in very tight pressure on fee structures for your work, and the ultimate revenues you generate being considerably less than you might have expected at first. Further, the industry is expected to become even more competitive in the next several years, placing even more pressure on moderators to give prospective clients a meaningful "reason why" they should hire them rather than the many alternative suppliers who are seeking to sell their services to your clients.

Pressure. As in most "consulting" fields, considerable pressures are placed on focus group moderators. The greatest source of pressure is the need to develop a clientele that will regularly use your services. Many new moderators have little or no experience or talent in sales and find it extremely difficult to carry out the ongoing selling effort needed to generate new clients and maintain existing ones. It is this pressure that motivates many moderators to leave the industry or to work for an organization that will provide them with research studies to implement regularly.

Moderators also face pressure to "deliver" the appropriate number of people for focus groups. If the recruiting organization is not successful in filling the participant quotas, the client will blame the moderator, who has the ultimate responsibility for managing the field aspects of a project. Therefore, as a moderator you face considerable pressure immediately before each session as you wait to see if your quota of participants arrives at the facility.

There is also great pressure to "perform" during sessions. Each focus group session is like the opening night of a new play, as the moderator does not know what the group will be like but is expected to achieve the research objectives with it. This pressure is intensified by the fact that client personnel are observing the proceedings from the back room, and some are very critical of any deviations from the norm. The moderator is expected to provide "interesting" groups, even if the topic being discussed is not particularly exciting. Many clients find observing focus groups to be very tedious and rely on the moderator to "perform" to make the sessions stimulating to watch.

Finally, moderators face the pressure of producing a quality final report in as short a time as possible. This is a source of extreme pressure for a busy moderator, as the reports must be written shortly after the groups are completed or they will back up, adding further pressure. Some moderators handle this problem by having junior people in their organization write their reports.

Running the Business. Independent moderators must also handle the administrative requirements of running a business. This includes seeing to such things as payroll, accounts receivable and payable, and tax filings.

Ways to Enter the Industry

If you have decided that a career as a moderator is appealing, your next step is to decide on the best approach to get into the field and begin to build a practice. Two very important considerations are involved here: the question of training, and the question of whether you should start out on your own or work for someone else.

Moderator Training

Since the publication of *The Practical Handbook and Guide to Focus Group Research* in 1987, the question I have been asked most often by people considering careers as moderators is what is the best way to get the training. Most people recognize the importance of good training but have little knowledge of their options in this regard. There are three principal paths that you might follow to become trained as a group moderator.

Apprenticing. In this very common path, a person learns how to moderate by working as a field coordinator for a successful moderator, observing the "mentor" in actual group situations as often as possible. Watching is part of the training here; depending on your relationship with your mentor, you might be able to moderate some groups under his or her supervision, then get his or her feedback about the strengths and weaknesses of your effort. You could also videotape your groups and conduct self-analyses of each of the sessions in order to perfect your skills. This can be an excellent way to learn moderating, if the individual to whom you are apprenticed has good basic skills *and* is willing to take the time to help you perfect your technique.

Training Courses. A few organizations provide formal training for people who wish to learn how to moderate focus groups. These courses normally last a few days and generally teach the basics of the process, including the role of the field service. The better courses offer "role playing" with real focus groups so that professionals can observe students conducting a session and then critique their performance. The best-known training course is offered by Burke Marketing Research of Cincinnati, Ohio, which runs several each year.

Working in Market Research. Many people become moderators after doing market research in a corporation or agency, in which they have been involved with focus groups from the perspective of the client. After observing enough groups from the back room to feel they understand how to conduct effective sessions, they go directly from the corporate or agency to an independent practice. Unfortunately, many of these moderators are not successful, as they quickly find that their skills as clients are quite different from those they need to moderate effectively. For a person considering a career as a moderator, working in a corporate or agency market research department can be an excellent way to get background. But unless they function as a moderator in this organization, it is unlikely that they will be qualified to go off on their own without further training.

Hanging out a Shingle. Many people who have an extensive background in marketing and are seeking to specialize choose not to seek *formal* training in focus group moderation; nor do they choose to apprentice with someone else, often because they feel these options would be demeaning to them in light of their recent position. Therefore even though they lack formal training, they hope that their prior marketing experience and industry contacts will enable them to gain clients. If you have a strong marketing background, are comfortable with the focus group process, *and* have a large number of contacts in the marketing and market research business, this can be an effective way to begin a career moderating focus groups. The biggest risk is that you will disappoint some of your first clients due to your lack of experience.

Starting on Your Own versus Working for Someone Else

In addition to your training considerations, you must decide whether you should start a focus group business on your own or work for someone else initially with the long-term goal of opening your own business. This is a very difficult decision for most people to make, as each option has very significant advantages and disadvantages.

Advantages of Working for Someone Else. The significant benefits associated with working for another organization before embarking on your own are as follows.

- You can learn how others conduct a business and can identify the strengths and weaknesses of their system in the process of developing your own plans. This will avoid your having to work on a "trial and error" basis when you do start out. For example, you can learn how to select the best facility, how to handle finances with the facility, what information the facility needs to recruit and to hold the groups, and about billing and collections relative to your clients and your field services.
- You can learn how to price your services. A project priced too low represents a lost profit opportunity, while one priced too high is probably lost business.
- You can develop important contacts with client organizations that will eventually become the basis for your own clientele. You might be encumbered by a noncompete

own clientele. You might be encumbered by a noncompete agreement when you go off on your own, the contacts you make while working for someone else will almost surely be essential to building your own practice.

- If you work for a good organization that is really interested in providing quality research, you can have the opportunity of getting supervision from more experienced people, which will result in your delivering a better overall product to your clients. Your long-term success as a moderator will depend on the quality of your own contacts.

In sum, working for someone else first gives you the opportunity to see how another person runs their business. This will be very helpful when you are faced with building your own. You may also prefer being an employee to being an entrepreneur. Not everyone is able to be a boss or own a company, carrying the responsibility of generating clients and running a business. Working for someone else's independent practice may help you realize that life in the corporate environment suits you fine after all.

Advantages of Working for Yourself. The most important benefits associated with operating your own business are as follows.

- Ventures are almost always much more rewarding financially for the boss or owner of the business. This is normally the most important reason why people begin their own businesses.
- You can control both your time and the type of clients you serve and try to attract the type of clients that are of interest to you. This can have a major impact on your overall happiness in the profession. You can also select the projects you will work on yourself and delegate the others to one of your employees or turn them down.
- You are in charge of the overall quality of the product that is delivered to your clients. Employees of companies can control only the quality of their *own* work, and the time they can allocate to each assignment may be limited. As the owner of the company, you can control (within reason) the quality of all the work you and your employees provide.
- There is ego gratification associated with running your own company. When the company becomes successful, you can

take the full credit for this achievement. For many people, this is the most important reason they want to be on their own.

Moderator Career Outline

Types of Moderators
  Self-employed full-time
  Self-employed part-time
  Employees of market research companies
  Employees of nonresearch companies
  Agency employees
  People between jobs
Advantages and Disadvantages
  Advantages
    Independence
    Self-dependence
    Ease of entry
    Low cost of entry
    Intellectual challenge
    Variety
    Professionalism
    Financial rewards
Disadvantages
    Extensive travel
    Night work
    Competitiveness
    Pressure
    Running the business
Ways to Enter the Industry
  Moderator training
    Apprenticing
    Training courses
    Working in market research
    "Hanging out a shingle"
  Starting on your own versus working for someone else
    Advantages of working for someone else
    Advantages of working for yourself

12

Building a Business Moderating Focus Groups

As we have seen, focus group research is a highly competitive field, with hundreds of moderators competing for business in every area of the country. Further, competitive bidding is on the increase, to keep costs at the lowest possible level. No longer does a moderator keep a client indefinitely as long as the quality of their work remains acceptable.

As a moderator seeking to build a practice, you need to understand the principles of establishing your own business, then be able to develop and execute a business plan that will achieve your objectives. This section provides guidelines to help you develop a business philosophy, then a plan of action.

Developing a Strategy

Perhaps the most significant problem that people have when they start their own service business is that they have not differentiated the service they offer from that of their competitors seeking the same clients. Before you begin your own business, you need to address the following principles so that your marketing programs will have maximum appeal to prospective clients.

Principle 1: Decide What You Have to Offer. You must identify your own strengths and weaknesses and determine what you offer that is different from—and ideally better than—what competing moderators offer. This self-assessment is both difficult and time-consuming, but if done properly, it will prove to be of significant value when you develop your marketing plans. Some of the things you might consider are:

- Your *technical* skills, such as prior experience with semiconductors, radio stations, or health and beauty products. These could be very important to a client seeking a moderator with experience in these areas.
- Your special *functional* skills, such as a prior career as a psychologist, salesperson, or line marketing executive. Some moderators effectively convince clients to use their services by virtue of their professional background.
- Your demographic experience, such as prior work in geriatrics, with children, with a certain ethnic group, and so on. Experience with specific demographic groups can be very important selling points for a moderator seeking to build a practice in a select market segment.
- Your bilingual capabilities. These can be very important to clients who are planning a series of focus groups with different ethnic groups but with the same moderator. At present there are very few well-known moderators who are capable of conducting focus groups in more than one language.
- Your educational background, including both formal education and background in the educational community. Some moderators with Ph.D.'s use their degree as the principal criterion that separates them from the competition. Other moderators who teach at the university level leverage that association as their key differentiating credential.

Principle 2: Determine What Types of Focus Groups You Feel Most Comfortable Moderating. This will impact significantly on your client solicitation efforts. You should define and list the types of focus groups that you are comfortable moderating, in which you can offer a meaningful "value added" service to your clients. Your list should be as specific as possible and should cover as many different situations as are appropriate for your skills. These are issues you should consider when determining the types of groups you can and cannot moderate:

- Groups with retail consumers versus business-to-business groups

- Groups of professionals, such as physicians, lawyers, architects, or engineers
- Product categories in which you have experience or expertise, and those you will not work with for personal reasons, such as tobacco or alcohol
- Demographic groups with whom you will and will not work; you might decide you are not qualified to work with children under ten or with adults over sixty-five, with various ethnic groups, and so on.

The key here is to develop parameters for the types of groups you feel most qualified to handle.

Principle 3: Develop Your Positioning. Essentially, a positioning means creating a "reason why" for your service that will distinguish you from your competition. This is probably the most important part of your marketing plan, as your chances of success are much greater if you can meaningfully communicate how you are different from your competition. Some people base their positioning on their prior experience (like their medical, technical, or sales background), which qualifies them for a certain type of clientele; others base it on their approach to conducting focus groups (that is, a practical, theoretical, or participative approach). Still others base it on such things as lower cost, faster speed, or better quality reports. The keys to an effective positioning are:

- It should be unique, identifying you as different from others in the business.
- It should provide a meaningful benefit to prospective clients.
- It should be easily understood.
- It should be permanent, a "positioning" that you are comfortable retaining for many years.

Principle 4: Develop a Service Philosophy. This involves establishing principles for your business for such areas as:

- how your clients will be serviced
- what your pricing policy will be
- what speed of report turnaround you will offer.

Building Awareness

Building a clientele for your business involves creating a business plan that outlines how you will generate clients. Many books have been written to help entrepreneurs write business plans, including my own *The Consultant's Manual; A Guide to Building a Successful Consulting Practice.* It is impossible to fully cover this topic here.

But *the first step in marketing any product or service is to generate awareness of it among your target audience.* You must therefore develop an awareness of your name among your prospective clients so that they will call you when a potential assignment develops. If you have not generated this awareness, moreover, a referral to you by a client's colleague will not be nearly as meaningful to them. Therefore, it is essential that you make awareness building a priority.

There are two major ways that service organizations build awareness of themselves: **direct** methods and **indirect** methods. Both of these are important for your service business.

Direct Methods

The three principal *direct* methods by which moderators market their practice, are direct mail, telemarketing, and advertising.

Direct Mail. This is the most common way that service companies develop awareness of their services, as it is relatively inexpensive and can be targeted specifically to the people who are the best prospects for their services. There are several different types of direct mail solicitations, each of which has its own advantages and disadvantages.

The first is *cold call letters,* or written communications that are sent to a targeted list of prospective clients, based on specific predetermined criteria. The clients on the list are not personally known to the sender. A moderator might develop a list of market research directors in companies that use focus groups and send them a cold call letter (perhaps with a brochure) introducing his or her services. The objective of the letter is to build awareness of the moderator's services, emphasizing why he or she should be considered the next time the prospective client plans a focus group research project. Moderators commonly use cold call letters in this way, as do focus group facilities, to alert moderators of their services.

But cold call letters are usually not particularly effective. Recipients often view them as junk mail and do not even read them unless they contain some very unusual or appealing element. On the other hand, sending multiple cold call letters to the same target individuals can generate a level of awareness for your organization that could ultimately generate new leads for you if the communications sent are well produced.

A more effective form of direct mail used to build awareness is the *quasi–cold call letter*. The quasi–cold call letter differs from the cold call letter in that it is not part of a mass mailing directed at a broad audience unknown to the sender, but rather a targeted mailing to people who have *some* knowledge of the sender or of a third party who endorses the sender. If an existing client, a friend, a business associate, or other contact gives you the names of some prospective clients, you can write them a letter indicating that "John Doe of Helpneed Company" suggested you communicate with them about the services you offer. This type of solicitation is dramatically more effective than a cold call letter, since the recipient has a meaningful point of reference—your referral source—that should increase the chances of reading your letter. Indeed, although the recipient does not know you, using a reference familiar to the recipient dramatically increases the likelihood that they will read your communication.

Both types of direct mail can be effective as a part of an overall awareness-building program, but you must follow them up with a telephone call if you hope to generate a prospective lead. *It is extremely unusual for a direct mail solicitation alone to result in a lead,* as virtually everyone who receives one waits for a follow-up call rather than take action themselves. The letter's purpose is to create some awareness and give you an excuse to make a telephone call, to introduce your services and hopefully set up a personal meeting.

Using direct mail (both cold and quasi–cold) in marketing has the advantage that you control it: the people who receive it, the timing, and the amount of money spent on it. Control of the timing is particularly important if you plan to follow up on the letters, as you can mail the letters on a schedule consistent with your plans and capabilities for following them up. It helps avoid the problem of not following up on a letter for several weeks due to the large number of follow-up calls that must be made.

Telemarketing. A second direct method of awareness building is telemarketing. This technique follows essentially the same principles as direct mail, in that you can either cold call prospective clients or use a third-party endorsement to get through to them.

Telemarketing has some advantages over direct mail that you should consider as you plan to market your focus group moderating services. The biggest advantage is that you will talk to prospective clients and therefore have the opportunity to personally "sell" your credentials to them on a one-to-one basis. It also gives the prospect the opportunity to ask you about your capabilities in relation to the needs of their organization. Because the communication is personal and one-on-one, you may be successful in convincing prospective clients to meet with you personally, where you can present your credentials and maybe even discuss a potential project.

Another major advantage of telemarketing is that you have complete control over the communication, the people who are contacted, and the number of calls made. This enables you to effectively manage the time and many you spend on these activities.

The disadvantages of telemarketing are threefold. First, it is very time-consuming. It can take up a large amount of time that might be used more productively in other types of awareness building. Second, it can be very difficult to get through to prospects, since most of them have secretaries or assistants who screen their calls. Third, the need to make long distance or toll calls to reach prospects can make it very expensive.

Advertising. The third direct method of awareness building is through paid advertising in newspapers, magazines, trade show brochures, and other vehicles. This can be an excellent approach if these guidelines are followed:

- The advertising contains a message that is *meaningful* to the target customers, *easy to understand,* and sufficiently *unique* in comparison to others. It should communicate your *positioning,* or the "reason why" someone should use your services. If your message does not have these qualities, your advertising is unlikely to be effective.

- You identify specific media capable of reaching a large percentage of your target audience. You might have an excellent message for prospective clients, but you must deliver it to them in such a way that awareness of your service will result.

- You must spend enough money on the media effort to expose your target customers to your advertising with sufficient frequency that it can generate awareness of your services. While it is impossible to say what the "right" amount of exposure—many different variables affect the "optimal" situation—as a very rough rule of thumb, your advertising should reach the target customers at least four times over a six-month period. This allows them to see the ad, read it, and maybe even remember its key points.

As a part of an awareness-building program, advertising can generate a broad reach of your message with much frequency. But the disadvantage of advertising is cost: the cost of a campaign strong enough to generate a meaningful level of awareness of your services can be considerable.

All these direct methods can help you build awareness of your service among your target prospects. The key is to develop a strategic plan that identifies the most appropriate role for them within your budgetary limitations.

Indirect Methods

Indirect methods of awareness building differ from direct methods in several respects.

- They generally do not require a *financial* investment by you but a commitment of your *time*.

- You do not have nearly as much control over the end result.

- They involve longer-term marketing activities to build awareness.

There are four principal indirect methods of generating awareness: public relations activities, publishing, teaching and seminars, and community involvement.

Public Relations Activities. This refers to activities that give publicity to your business in media that reach your target customers. One of the most effective forms of public relations is to be quoted as an expert or to be the subject of a story in trade publications that reach your target customers. These publications tend to be read relatively thoroughly by the "right" people. Most people in service businesses are very skeptical about the success they would have in using publicity to help generate awareness. They do not feel their service is sufficiently newsworthy to generate publicity. A focus group moderator can do several things to realize meaningful public relations for their service.

- *Conduct a focus group for free for a volunteer organization* such as the Red Cross, the United Way, or your town government. If the topic is sufficiently meaningful, you should be able to motivate a local newspaper or TV or radio station to publish the findings. Mention of your work in local media can effectively reach target customers in your area and help raise their awareness of your services.
- *Become involved in a trade organization* (either in market research or in a specific industry), and do a project for it that will result in publicity in the trade media. You might conduct a focus group among the members of an industry group aimed at identifying trends in the industry for the next few years. Trade publications like to publish this type of information, as it is of interest to almost all their members.
- Leverage the local or trade press whenever you can. Seek appropriate media to provide coverage before, during, or after any speeches you give, positions you accept in trade or community organizations, courses you teach at the local high school or college, and the like. The objective is to get your name in the media as much as possible by alerting them to all newsworthy activities in which you are involved.

In summary, you must always be thinking about ways to interest the press in your activities so it will cover your efforts. You must view this as a long term effort, but one to which you make a commitment on an ongoing basis. It can take a long time to see the results of public relations, but the payoff can be very beneficial in awareness of and leads for your services.

Publishing. One of the best ways to build awareness for your business is to publish articles in appropriate publications about topics related to focus groups. In my experience, it is beneficial to use both horizontal and vertical publications. *Horizontal publications* are those that are not industry specific but are aimed at marketing managers, market research professionals, ad agency account executives, and the like. *Vertical publications* are those that are industry specific, such as *Bank Marketing, Television/Radio Age,* and so on. Publishing articles in both vertical and horizontal publications is an excellent way to become known in your industry and to build your credibility with your target customers. Further, the articles that you publish can be very effective inserts in direct mail efforts, and excellent "leave-behinds" when you make a presentation to a prospective client.

To effectively use this method of building awareness, you should commit yourself to a writing schedule that enables you to publish an article in a significant trade publication four to six times each year. You may find it difficult to get articles published—most magazines have more submissions than they can use—so it is generally necessary to submit your work to several different publications in order to have it accepted by one of them.

Teaching and Seminars. Another excellent way to build awareness is to teach a course in market research at a local adult education program or nearby university. This provides instant credibility for you and establishes you as an expert in your field among both the people in your classes and those who become aware of your academic activities. Teaching a course can also be an excellent source of client referrals, since students often are working for companies that might need your services.

Another excellent way to generate awareness is to give speeches and participate in discussion panels at trade meetings and conventions. This gives you excellent exposure to your target customers and will likely position you as an expert in your field with the people in your audience. It is not easy to be selected to speak at trade meetings, since many people are also trying to communicate with these audiences. But if you adopt a long-term view, you can work your way into organizations over time and be considered when public speaking opportunities arrive that are appropriate for you.

Community Involvement. Another indirect method of awareness building is to become involved in community organizations where you can gain exposure to potential clients. People who are successful in business also tend to be involved at the local level in various organizations, as a way to "give something back to the community." Such organizations are an excellent place to meet people on a semi-social level whom you might have great difficulty reaching at their office.

The key to this approach is to get to know as many people as possible in the organization *and* to take a leadership role in it. Try to contribute to the organization something related to marketing and/or focus groups, so that the other people in the organization will appreciate your "professional" capabilities and may become interested in working with you.

It is important, however, that you not join these groups with the explicit objective of selling yourself to the members and generating leads. This type of behavior can work to your detriment and will reduce your chances for success. The business contacts you make in community organizations should come as a result of recognition for your excellent work for them.

Indirect methods of awareness building offer some very important advantages over direct methods. One is the *cost* which is generally either free or very low. You can implement many different indirect efforts without expending significant funds. Another advantage is that indirect methods tend to give greater credibility and believability than direct methods, because of the third-party endorsement that is implied in media coverage, speakers engagements, and community recognition.

An important disadvantage of indirect methods is your lack of control over the frequency, timing, and content of the messages that result from them. Unlike paid advertising, telemarketing, and direct mail, it is not normally possible to determine when (or if) you will get coverage in the trade press, or when (or where) you will get articles published. Indeed, the difficulty of gaining publication, securing prestigious speaking engagements, and being elected to positions in key trade organizations is another disadvantage of indirect methods. They can be very effective *if* you can get them. Since many people in service organizations realize the importance of indirect methods, the competition is often fierce, and success requires a long time and much effort on your part. Many people who run service companies are unwilling to make such a long-term effort and give up before they realize the rewards of these methods.

Still another disadvantage is the time involved in writing articles and speeches, in participating in industry or community associations. Many people in service businesses are unwilling to invest so much time in an activity that is not guaranteed to generate them new business in the short term.

Selling Your Services

Nothing happens until a sale is made. You can have the most effective marketing program possible for your focus group moderating business, but if you do not succeed in selling a prospective client on using *you,* your efforts to generate awareness will be wasted. You may not consider yourself a salesperson, but your success as a focus group moderator will be directly proportional to your effectiveness as a salesperson. This section covers the key elements in selling your services to prospective clients: generating qualified leads, presenting your credentials to prospects, using brochures and leave-behinds, and writing proposals.

Generating Leads

In most service organizations, the biggest problem that management faces is generating qualified leads. Without leads, you have no clients, and without clients, you have no moderating practice. You could be the best moderator in the industry, but if you do not have an active program to continuously generate leads, your business will not prosper.

Awareness Building. One very important way to generate leads is your awareness-building program, using the direct and indirect methods discussed earlier in this chapter. A successful program will not only increase overall awareness of your capabilities but will motivate some prospects to contact you, especially people who have heard you speak at a seminar or trade meeting, read something you published, or met you at a community or trade organization meeting.

Satisfied Clients. The most valuable source of leads for your business is satisfied clients for whom you have previously provided moderating services. These clients understand the type and quality of services you provide and may well refer you to others in need of a moderator. They give you not only a referral but an excellent reference. Most successful service business owners establish a personal goal of securing at least two or three qualified leads from each client they serve successfully. Yet most people in the service business are reluctant to use their existing clients as lead sources, since they feel it could be an irritant to them and they do not want to risk damaging an existing relationship. But in my experience, most satisfied clients are happy to pass along names of prospective clients to service providers, as they feel they are taking a positive action on the provider's behalf.

Direct Mail. Direct mail to a targeted list of qualified prospects is another excellent source of leads. You should develop a mailing list of all prospective clients for your service and update it regularly as you identify new people. The best way to use this list is to mail something to them three or four times a year—something directly related to your services but that is not a "heavy sales" piece. It could be an article you have published, a story about you in a publication, or the findings of a "generic" research study you have implemented. If the pieces you send out are of interest to the prospects, they may generate leads for you that will result in new clients.

Facility Relationships. Another fertile source of leads are your local focus group research facilities. It is in your best interest to generate meaningful relationships with these organizations as their clients often ask them for references of qualified moderators. Identify the facilities that you will be using regularly, and concentrate as much business as possible in them. By becoming a regular with them, they will be more likely to consider you when they get asked for referrals.

The same is true for industry trade associations. Cultivating a good relationship with several of these can result in referrals for you later on.

Presenting Your Credentials

Like most new service businesses, you will likely be asked to make presentations to prospective clients to give them an overview of the services you provide, your capabilities, and your costs. Many independent moderators do not take this process very seriously, as they do not view themselves as salespeople and object to having to "sell" themselves. This can be a fatal mistake, particularly given the heavily competitive nature of the focus group business at present.

Therefore you should welcome the opportunity to present your credentials to a prospective client—precisely *because* it gives you the chance to sell your services. The most important part of your credentials presentation is your account of the "unique point of difference" you offer, as against your competition. It is essential, as we have seen, that you position yourself—that you identify a specific element of your service, your background, or your approach that differentiates you from the competition in your marketing effort. Your positioning should be the focus of your credentials presentation, and the "story" you tell throughout your presentation must support this point. Examples of positioning that moderators can use effectively are shown in the chart, grouped according to strategic approaches. These are intended only as examples of specific ways you could communicate your positioning to prospective clients. There are an unlimited number of alternatives, based on your assessment of your own strengths and on your perception of the market.

These are some guidelines that you might want to consider in determining your positioning. It must:

- be meaningful to your target customers
- be consistent with your capabilities
- be memorable and easy to understand—very simple and directly to the point—so it can deliver your message in milliseconds

TABLE 12–1
Positioning

Strategic Approach	Intent
Demographic Approaches: • focus groups with young kids • broad-based experience with the elderly • know how to communicate with the medical community	These position the moderator as a specialist in working with selected groups of consumers.
Technical Approaches: • specialist in using projective techniques to delve a little deeper • focus groups that are quantifiable • focus groups that generate new product concepts	These address specific uses of focus groups by the client. As technical approaches they will work across demographic lines.
Full Service Approaches: • turn-key focus group research • specialist in not only focus groups but one-on-ones and dyads • complete research capability offers the best in qualitative and quantitative research	These present you as servicing all the needs of the clients in the qualitative and perhaps in the quantitative research areas.

- be different from that of your competition
- be easily incorporated into the various communication materials you develop

Your credentials presentation may be the only opportunity you will have to sell yourself to a prospective client. The information you communicate in it must therefore be thorough, in order to address all the questions the client might have, and it must also effectively sell your unique benefits over those of the competition. The ideal presentation of your focus group credentials should contain the following:

- *An overview of the services you provide.* You should indicate whether your service includes such activities as selection of the facility, coordinating with the facility, recruiting the participants, presentation of a final report, and preparation of written transcripts of the session.

- *Your background and credentials.* This basically involves communicating your resume (or curriculum vitae), providing such information as your educational background, job history, other experience related to the prospect's needs, publications, and key positions you have held (or currently hold) in relevant industry groups.
- *Your unique point of difference as against others in the business.* This is your "positioning," with appropriate information supporting your claim for your positioning.
- *Your approach to moderating.* This includes general costs, scheduling, and your relationship with facilities. It is not possible to provide prospective clients with a "rate card" for focus groups, but there are some meaningful points that you can communicate, such as the range of costs for your groups, and the timing with which you traditionally operate, in terms of developing the guide, holding the groups, and providing the final report.
- *Your previous clients and category experience.* It is extremely important to communicate the different types of assignments you have had and clients you have serviced. To some prospective clients, this is the most important part of any credentials presentation.

Your presentation should be flexible in format, allowing for and accommodating a one-on-one meeting in addition to a small group if necessary. It is advisable to produce your presentation both in a flipchart format (for one-on-one meetings) and in a slide or overhead projector format for larger meetings.

Using Brochures and Leave-Behinds

In my experience, brochures are much overemphasized in the business plans of new source businesses. It is almost standard practice for someone starting out as a moderator to develop a brochure as the *first* part of his or her marketing program, as it is presumably an essential step in generating clients. And to be sure, it is often desirable to have a brochure to leave behind with prospects after a meeting or to mail to someone seeking information about your services you offer. But my experience suggests that it is not necessary even to have a brochure to build a successful moderating business. This is not to say that you should not develop a brochure. Rather, you should concentrate more on other aspects of your awareness-building and marketing programs first, as they will normally contribute more to your ultimate success than a brochure.

Rather than develop a "formal" brochure, many moderators and other source consultants simply create a one-or-two-page synopsis of their credentials presentation and use that as a handout for meetings or to send to prospects seeking information about their services. As attachments to this brief piece, some people add copies of articles they have written or press coverage they have received.

Writing Proposals

The final part of your selling process is to develop a proposal that you can provide to prospective clients following your credentials presentation. The objective of this document is to induce the prospect to use your services to achieve their research objectives for a specific research project. There are many different ways to write a proposal, but as a general rule, an effective proposal contains the following specific elements:

Background. The statement of background communicates your understanding of the prospective client's situation and the reason they have asked for your involvement. Importantly, it should state the research objectives, if known, and the intended use of the results.

Methodology. The description of the approach that you will employ for the focus groups should include such things as:

- the number of groups you recommend
- the location of the groups
- the proposed timing
- the screening criteria for the participants, and the way they will be recruited (that is, by random telephone calls, lists you provide the facility, facility database, or the like)
- a brief overview of the subject matter that you will cover in the groups
- The type of *report* you will provide
- The *costs* of conducting the groups, including incidental costs such as travel and external stimuli

Process. The discussion of the *process* you will employ should cover such things as:

- the need for a briefing to provide you with background on the topic being researched
- writing the moderator guide, and the role of the client organization in this effort
- the development of a screening questionnaire, and the need for the client to review it to ensure full agreement with the screening criteria

Closing. The close is essentially a brief statement indicating your interest in working with the prospective client on this project and your need for their approval to proceed by a specific date, in order to deliver the research "product" by the timing identified in the proposal.

Credentials Review. Finally, the proposal should summarize your credentials and the principal reasons why the prospective client should hire you to do the research.

Servicing Clients

One of the most important aspects of building a successful focus group research business is to develop a group of clients who are happy with your work and continue to retain you for most or all of their research projects. These clients can also be important sources of new business leads for you and references for prospective clients who are interested in learning about your work.

Developing successful client relationships involves more than producing an excellent research "product." Many people are capable of moderating effectively and writing excellent reports. Often what will single you out from your competition is the *service* you provide to your clients. You should be aware of several major components of customer service to build effective and long-lasting relationships with your clients. These components are as follows.

Personal Involvement

A key component of effective client service is to get to know the people in the client organization who are involved with your research project. This builds a relationship in which you are more than just one of several focus group "vendors" who serve the client. This *does not* mean that you do significant amounts of client entertaining or gifts to your clients; rather, it means that you develop a personal relationship with the key client people and show a genuine interest in them as "people" rather than merely as sources of income. It may be desirable to "break bread" with your clients on an occasional basis and to interact personally in a relaxed environment, many successful relationships have been built without any entertainment.

My experience is that business relationships that develop beyond day-to-day business interactions tend to become stronger, more important, and more productive for both parties. Further, your work will be more enjoyable if you have meaningful relationships with the people with whom you are working.

Maintaining Regular Contact

You should stay in touch with your clients throughout the focus group process to keep them up to date on all important details. This is particularly important during the recruitment of participants— it may be necessary to change the screening criteria if recruitment difficulties arise, such as relaxing product usage requirements, changing the income level or age group, or paying more co-op so that more qualified participants are willing to attend. These types of decisions should be made only with the agreement of the client, since they are deviations from the original agreed-upon plan. I find that it helps to make contact with the key client personnel every two or three days after recruiting starts, so they are aware of the progress being made.

Availability

A key customer service provided by a moderator is his or her availability to clients. This involves being willing to juggle your own schedule to meet the client's scheduling needs for the groups, the briefing session, and the presentation of the final report. It also involves being available to meet with your client throughout the preparation of the guide and to answer the client's telephone calls to you. One of the biggest complaints that clients have about moderators is that they are not available to talk to them when they call, to give them reports on the recruitment process, to answer their questions about drafts of the guide, or to give them directions to the facility.

Responsiveness

It is also essential to be responsive to clients' needs, so they feel you are taking care of them well. Responsiveness means:

- Returning their phone calls promptly. A client should never have to wait more than a half day to hear from you after leaving a phone message in your office.
- Responding quickly to their need for internal meetings or discussions about the moderator guide or screening questionnaire.
- Answering their questions quickly and thoroughly, showing them that their issues are important to you and that you recognize they are important to them—even if they are actually very minor issues.

Speed

A major client complaint about focus group moderators is that they do not appreciate the client's sense of urgency about implementing the groups and getting the final report. Focus groups are often selected as the research methodology used because information needed for a decision can be gathered from them quickly. You should be very sensitive to the timing needs of your client and make the extra sacrifice necessary to produce the final report promptly. Most organizations want the report quickly, so that there will be one "official" position on what occurred during the sessions rather than having many different stories representing the interpretations of the attendees go around the company. As a general rule, I try to complete a report within three to five working days of the final session.

Measuring Client Satisfaction

Most moderators understand that the objective of a client relationship is to have happy clients who are pleased with their work. But only a very few moderators do anything to monitor the level of their clients' satisfaction. When the topic of client satisfaction is raised with moderators who do not formally monitor it, they normally indicate that they are "in regular contact with their clients and therefore know how they feel." This is probably true in a lot of situations, but it is still an excellent and highly recommended policy to *formally* monitor the level of your clients' satisfaction.

An excellent way to do this is to send a brief questionnaire to your client immediately after the completion of a focus group project. The objective of this questionnaire is to determine their level of satisfaction with:

- the moderator guide
- the moderation of the groups
- the performance of the facility in recruitment, physical plant, food, and the like
- the quality of the final report
- the timing of the groups and the final report.

The questionnaire should also ask for their overall satisfaction (perhaps on a five-point scale). This will help you track your performance over time, both in the absolute and on a client-by-client basis.

Finally, your questionnaire should ask the client for suggestions about what you can do to provide a higher level of service to them. This type of input could motivate you to change some of your processes.

Summary

For many people, focus group moderating is a very exciting career option. It offers them significant freedom, gives them control over their own time, and provides them with the chance to make a very significant income. But success as a moderator requires you to develop a plan of action for your business, including such things as:

- Developing positioning, or a unique point of difference for your services in contrast to your competition
- Identifying target customers based on your positioning
- Developing awareness of your services by an ongoing effort involving direct and indirect methods

- Creating the tools necessary to sell your services to prospective clients, especially a simple presentation that will clearly articulate the benefits of your services for clients
- Effectively servicing your clients so they consider you a regular provider of focus group services.

Adhering to the principles outlined in this chapter and the one before will help you succeed in creating a focus group moderating business that will provide you with both personal gratification and financial rewards.

Building a Business Outline

Developing a Strategy
   Decide what you have to offer
   Determine what types of groups you are most comfortable moderating
   Develop your positioning
   Develop a service philosophy
Building Awareness
   Direct methods
      Direct mail
      Telemarketing
      Advertising
   Indirect methods
      Public relations activities
      Publishing
      Teaching and seminars
      Community involvement
Selling Your Services
   Generating leads
      Awareness building
      Satisfied clients
      Direct mail
      Facility relationships
   Presenting your credentials
   Using brochures and leave-behinds
   Writing proposals
Servicing Clients

Personal involvement
Maintaining regular contact
Availability
Responsiveness
Speed
Measuring Client Satisfaction

13

The Role of the Facility

One of the most important elements in focus group research is the organization hired to hold the groups, normally referred to as the facility, the field service, or the local market research company. In this book we call this organization the facility. Most experienced moderators agree that even an extremely well-run facility cannot make up for poorly conceived or badly moderated research project. But a poorly run facility can easily ruin the best of projects. This chapter discusses the role of the facility in focus group research and identifies specific actions that a moderator can take to improve the chances of having a successful experience with a facility.

The term *focus group facility* can mean different things, depending on the resources such an organization provides. In this book a focus group facility constitutes the link between the client, the moderator, and the participants in the groups.

The Services of the Facility

Facilities offer many different services for their clients. How much a client uses these various services depends on the needs of the specific research project, the sophistication of the client, and the specific capabilities of the facility. My experience in conducting hundreds of groups over the past fifteen years at dozens of facilities across the United States and Canada has shown me that there is a wide range of capabilities among facilities. Some are extremely well run and very client oriented, while others are operated like "Mom and Pop" businesses and do not understand what is required to hold successful group sessions.

The following is a brief overview of the most common functions that facilities perform.

Participant Recruitment

The participants in most focus group sessions have been directly recruited by a facility or by a local subcontractor that works with a facility. Some moderators do not use facilities for recruiting—they feel that an independent recruiter whom they manage will find better quality respondents, or a comparable quality at lower cost. In this chapter we will assume that the facility has responsibility for the recruiting.

Recruiting Procedures. The most important responsibility of the focus group facility is to ensure that the correct participants are included in the sessions. They should be obtained through procedures that have been agreed to in advance by either the client or the moderator and the facility. Normally, these procedures involve:

- Eliminating frequent participants in focus groups. For consumer groups, most moderators do not want participants who have been in a focus group in the previous six months. (This guideline is often waived for professional groups, due to the smaller number of prospective participants.) The reason for this is that participants who are regularly involved in focus groups tend to try to anticipate the wishes of the moderator and respond to the questions as an "authority" rather than as a regular consumer.
- Ensuring (to the best of their ability) that the people in the group do not know each other. Some facilities try to "cheat" the system and ask prospective participants for the names of friends who meet the general screening criteria and who might be willing to come to the group. But this should never be done, since participants who know each other may have relationships or a pecking order that impacts on the quality of the group output. Experience shows that participants often respond differently to questions when they are in the presence of someone they know, as opposed to strangers.
- Ensuring that each participant is qualified, based on his or

her responses to the questions in the screening questionnaire, without any prompting from the recruiter. Some research projects require participants who have very specific demographic characteristics, psychographic measurements, or product usage behavior; the incidence of qualified people in the population maybe very limited. A facility's recruiters may become frustrated by the difficulty in finding qualified participants and may "bend" the requirements or prompt the prospective participants to improve the chances of his or her qualifying. This is a clear violation of the "contract" between the facility and the client.

- Ensuring that sufficient participants have been recruited so that a full complement is present when a group begins. Virtually all facilities recruit about 20 percent more people than they need for the sessions (that is, twelve for a group of ten) to account for "no shows."

Ensuring Attendance. The facility is responsible for confirming that each person who has agreed to come to the group will participate within twenty-four hours of the session. For evening groups, attendance is normally confirmed on the morning of same day. It is a major embarrassment for both the facility and the moderator when the required number of people do not come for the sessions.

Providing Directions. The facility is responsible for providing the participants with correct and easy-to-read directions to get to the facility and instructing them to arrive at least fifteen minutes before the start of the session. The facility must take into consideration the traffic of people in its physical plant and account for that when providing instructions to participants. Participants should not arrive late if the facility has properly informed them of the details associated with getting to the session.

Rescreening Participants

It is the responsibility of the facility to administer a brief rescreening questionnaire to the people when they arrive to ensure that they are appropriate participants. This should include the principal screening questions that were originally administered when they were recruited. For a group with particularly difficult recruiting parameters, the client should provide the facility with a new series of questions to ensure that the recruiters selected the proper people to participate in the groups.

Physical Plant

The facility's physical plant is extremely important in focus groups research. It can contribute meaningfully to the success or failure of a research project. Some of the key characteristics of an effective physical plant include:

Reception Area. The facility should have a reception area for greeting participants that is away from the area where the sessions are held. This is important for noise control in the facility and so that the participants leaving one group do not meet those waiting for the next session. It also allows the client observers to arrive anonymously, which becomes important if they are celebrities or public figures and might be recognized by the participants.

Focus Group Room. The facility must have a focus group room that is sufficiently large and well appointed that the moderator and the participants are comfortable. A session can be ruined if the room is crowded or hot or has poor acoustics.

The focus group room must be soundproofed so that noises from the street or the other parts of the facility do not intrude. Most facilities do not fully understand this and have not taken the appropriate actions to keep the rooms as isolated from noise interruptions as possible.

Observation Room. The back room must be comfortable and provide appropriate viewing space so that the client observers can see the proceedings easily. The one-way mirror must be large, the chairs for the observers must be comfortable, and the sound system must allow the observers to hear each of the participants, even if they speak in a very low voice.

Restrooms. Adequate restroom facilities must be nearby so that client observers and participants are not out of their rooms for an extended period of time.

Appropriate Support Materials

The facility is responsible for:

- Having chair rails on outer shelves in the focus group room, to enable the moderator to display external stimuli during the sessions.
- Having a sturdy easel pad and adequate markers in the focus group room, so the moderator can write directions to the participants or record their responses, as necessary.
- Providing pencils and notepads at each place around the table, so the participants can write things down according to the directions of the moderator.
- Making legible nametags for the participants and the moderator that show the name by which each individual *likes to be called* (as opposed to their full name as collected on the screener). This requires a little extra work, as the facility personnel must ask each what name they want to be called by the moderator.

Audio and/or Video Support

All focus groups are audiotaped, and a large percentage are also videotaped. The facility must provide a quality system to produce tapes that will capture the proceedings for those unable to attend.

In the case of videotaping, two options are available at present. One is a fixed camera, which is turned on when the group begins and is not moved during the session. Normally it does not require an operator and is usually offered free or at a very nominal charge by the facility. The other option is hiring a camera operator who runs the camera during the group, panning and focusing in on various participants while they are talking. This arrangement provides for a much higher quality videotape but is significantly more expensive than the fixed camera option. This alternative is generally selected when the videotape is to be used for a formal presentation following the group sessions.

Food for the Participants and Clients

The facility is responsible for providing food to those involved in the groups. Chapter 6 of *The Practical Handbook and Guide to*

Focus Group Research discussed food requirements for different times of day and should be consulted when planning for sessions. The important consideration here is that the facility should take the initiative in discussing the food requirements with the client. Some clients have very specific food needs (such as kosher, vegetarian, no alcoholic beverages, and the like), and the facility must be very sensitive to these needs and provide the right food.

Facility personnel should also be available to the observers and participants during the session to ensure that adequate food and drink are always available.

Assurance of Confidentiality

Confidentiality is a very sensitive area for most clients as they want to maintain the highest degree of security about the content of their research. To this end, the facility must ensure that:

- Competitive organizations are not conducting groups in the facility at the same time.
- The facility employees respect the confidentiality of all projects and do not reveal the names of clients conducting groups or the topics of the groups to anyone.
- All special materials used during the session must be returned to the client or destroyed after the group. Even an apparently innocuous piece of paper left behind in a focus group room could be very damaging to a client if it fell into the wrong hands.
- All external stimuli to be used during a session must be stored in a secure place before the session begins. Client organizations quite commonly send materials to a facility in advance to ensure that they will be available during the group. These materials should not be seen by anyone other than authorized personnel of the facility and client personnel.

Financial and Administrative Requirements

These responsibilities include:

- Remunerating the participants (that is, making co-op payments) for participating in the groups and properly documenting that they have been paid. This is important to ensure proper financial reporting to the client organization; it could also become important at a later date as a record of the participants in the sessions.

- Securing signed releases from participants, if the client requires this. For some product categories (like food, alcoholic beverages, and smoking products) it is often advisable to obtain a release from the participants *before* they are included in the session.
- Cooperating with the client organization to establish the most appropriate co-op payment to the participants. This is one area of focus group research where the client and the facility are often working at odds. The client wants to keep the co-op as low as possible, while the facility wants to offer a higher co-op to make recruiting easier and improve its own profit margin. The optimal solution is to set a co-op level that enables both organizations to meet their financial objectives.
- Providing fast and accurate billing to the appropriate client personnel after the groups. The payers should not have to wait more than two weeks to get a bill for the session—less the co-op advance, which is normally sent in advance.

Miscellaneous Responsibilities

The better focus group facilities provide their clients with some or all of the following services. For those that require meaningful time of the facility staff, it is acceptable for the facility to charge the client an appropriate fee.

Photocopying. Often a moderator or client observes require photocopies of pages or documents while at the facility. This service should be provided at a nominal cost.

Telephone and Fax Services. The facility should provide telephones to the client personnel so they can make and receive calls. Any toll calls or faxes are expected to be funded by the caller.

Sample Product Pickup. Sometimes the moderator asks the facility to obtain samples of local products for use during the groups. This can be very important to a moderator in an "out of town" situation where specific brands are not available anywhere but in the location where the groups are being held. Most facilities charge an hourly rate, plus the product cost, for securing such product samples.

Product Disposal. At the completion of a series of groups, it is not unusual for the facility to be asked to discard test products so they do not have to be transported back to the home office. The facility is responsible for disposing these items without letting them get into the hands of the public. Giving in to any temptation to keep them or give them to friends or colleagues would be a breach of security on the part of the facility.

Moderator Recommendations. It is relatively common for facilities to be asked to recommend a moderator to companies seeking to conduct focus groups. Well run facilities retain the names of several qualified moderators that can be provided when clients ask for them.

Hotel and Restaurant Recommendations and Reservations. People attending focus groups in out-of-town locations often ask for hotel and restaurant recommendations. The facility should retain this type of information and provide it to clients as needed. If asked, the facility should make local phone calls to handle reservations for the requesting party.

Common Problems at Facilities

It is necessary for moderators to understand the problems they are likely to encounter with facilities so they can take appropriate actions to avoid them. The most common problems relate to the facility, the recruitment, and the costs.

Facility Problems

Problems with facilities typically involve the physical plant, the noise level, and the staff quality. Each of these can significantly reduce the quality of the research, and the moderator must therefore anticipate them before a facility is contracted.

The most obvious way a moderator can avoid these problems is to ask other moderators about their experiences with the facility. Almost any full-time moderator will give a colleague an honest appraisal of a facility where he or she has worked. This process can help a moderator find a facility that is reasonably acceptable for a research project.

Room Quality. Even in the best facilities, some rooms are better than others, in terms of size, decor, amenities, or soundproofing. Moderators can avoid being assigned unacceptable rooms by identifying the rooms they want for their sessions at the time they reserve space at the facility. Since most moderators do not reserve specific rooms, it is almost always possible for those who do have a preference to reserve the space they desire.

Noise Level. The problem of noise can significantly hamper the focus group process. Ideally, the focus group room should be isolated from all outside noises, including street sounds, noise from other parts of the building, and noise from the facility itself. The existence of the first two makes it extremely difficult for a moderator to continue to use a facility. Facility owners can eliminate outside noise by soundproofing the walls, windows, and ceiling of the rooms. Although outside noise is a relatively common problem at facilities, it bothers some people more than others. Often a problem exists but the facility management is unaware of it since it has not been brought to their attention. My experience is that most facility owners want to be told about problems of this type so they can correct them, rather than have moderators use alternative locations.

Sounds coming from within the facility can be very distracting to groups and can inhibit discussion. The most common cause of this is facility employees who are not sensitive to the need for quiet during sessions. It is often necessary for moderators to communicate with facility management beforehand and get their assurance that employees will be sensitive to the need for quiet. Further, moderators must often remind the hostess on duty at the sessions that there must be absolute quiet. I have often had to leave the room during a session to alert facility employees about the distraction they are causing. If noise continues to be a problem, it is necessary to change facilities.

Recruitment Problems

The second major problem area that moderators experience is in the recruiting of participants. In this category are improperly qualified participants, "professional" respondents used to fill the group quota, participants who show up late for sessions, and an insufficient number of participants. Moderators can take some actions to minimize these problems, but it is often necessary to change facilities to really correct them. Another option is to contract the recruiting to an outside organization that specializes in recruiting, thereby taking the facility out of the loop in this matter. This is generally not the best solution, however, as it requires the moderator to do more logistical coordination to arrange for sessions. It also reduces the facility's incentive work with the moderator since it makes much less money than it would if it were also responsible for recruitment. The following are suggested ways that moderators can work out the problems with a facility rather than take the recruiting to an outside service.

No-Shows. The moderator's first action is to identify the specific nature of the problem. Suppose the problem is unacceptably high percentage of "no-shows"—the moderator contracted for ten qualified participants but only six were present. The facility manager's typical response is that all the people were confirmed that day, and the facility has no control over those who decide not to come at the last minute. But "no-shows" are generally not a problem at the better-run facilities because their recruiters do a better job of determining whether a confirmation is sincere. Also, they overrecruit by two to four people so that the client is not disappointed by no-shows.

To correct a no-show problem at a facility, the moderator should ensure that more people are being recruited than are needed. He or she may also inform the facility that if the minimum number of participants do not show up, significant payment penalties will be instituted.

Unqualified Participants. The second recruitment problem is unqualified participants. This is a very serious problem, as a session with people who have not been correctly recruited is unlikely to be productive. A focus group to identify the best positioning for a diet soft drink will probably not be useful unless the participants are consumers of diet soft drinks. A focus group on a new service offered by a foreign car manufacturer will not be very productive if the participants all drive American cars.

The moderator should take great pains to ensure that the right people are recruited for the sessions by doing several things. First, the moderator should explain to the facility management the needs for the session, ensuring that they fully understand what type of people are to be recruited. Second, he or she should provide the facility with a screening questionnaire that their recruiters can use to select participants. Many moderators do not take the initiative to prepare a questionnaire and instead rely on the facility to translate their verbal instructions into an appropriate questionnaire. But to get the right people, the moderator must write the questionnaire.

The moderator can also ask the facility to provide a spreadsheet that summarizes key data about the people it has recruited. These are typically prepared three to four days before the groups, and they include the respondents' first names and their answers to the key screening questions. By getting this sheet before the sessions, the moderator can determine whether the correct people have been recruited and change in the composition of the group before it is too late.

The moderator's final control is to require the facility to rescreen the participants when they arrive for the group. This involves asking them the three or four key questions from the screening questionnaire once again. This often eliminates a respondent who was coerced to come by an interviewer who was trying to fill the quota and was not as thorough as he or she should have been.

Some moderators take another step; they start the discussion by asking the participants a few screening questions to ensure that they qualify. This can be part of the warm-up discussion and is often an excellent way to ensure that the composition of the group is correct.

"Professional" Respondents. "Professional" respondents are those who regularly participate in focus group sessions, often as many as two or more per week. Some facilities are significantly less professional than others and are not as discriminating in recruitment. They will use "professionals" to fill difficult quotas or simply to make their recruiting faster and therefore more profitable.

Most moderators and clients do not want these people in their groups because they do not provide the "fresh" responses that other participants do. Most screening questionnaires try to eliminate people who have participated in a focus group in the previous six months; but this process is not foolproof, as it is impossible to know if the respondent is telling the truth.

It is very difficult to eliminate "professional" respondents from a group, particularly if they have been briefed about the need to act like a fresh respondent. Some moderators try to search them out during the warm-up discussion, feeling that they will sometimes give themselves away inadvertently.

The problem of "professional" respondents is of sufficient concern to the research industry that there is an organization—Sigma Research—that collects data from moderators concerning the names and addresses of participants in their groups. Three or four days before a session, a moderator send Sigma the list of people who have been recruited by the facility, and a computer search is conducted to determine whether any of them have been reported as participating in the recent past. While this will not be a foolproof system unless all moderators and facilities participate in it, it is presently the best option available. Such organizations will probably become more important to the qualitative research industry over the next few years as the need for fresh respondents become more important to the research.

Late Arrivals. In some facilities, it is not uncommon for half or more of the participants to arrive ten or twenty minutes after a session is supposed to begin. Most moderators do not want to start a group until they have at least seven or eight participants, so if sufficient people are not present, they must wait for more to arrive and start the group late. This causes valuable time to be lost. Moreover, if a moderator permits late-arriving participants in the room, it can be very disruptive to the discussion.

There are a few actions that moderators can take to minimize the lateness problem. First, they should instruct the screener to tell the participants to arrive at the facility fifteen minutes before the group is expected to begin. Therefore, a participant for a six o'clock session is told to arrive at five forty-five. In most cases, this will significantly reduce late arrivals.

The second thing moderators can do is to alert the facility that they will not pay co-op to any participant who arrives at the facility more than five minutes after the group is scheduled to begin. This will motive the facility to get the participants to arrive on time, so that it will not have to turn latecomers away without pay. The facility has an interest in keeping its respondents happy, as it wants to be able to use them again in the future. Also, they do not want to develop a bad reputation in the community that would preclude prospective participants from coming to their sessions. If a moderator institutes a no-pay policy for latecomers, the facility will be forced to pay them from its budget so as not to alienate them.

Pricing Problems

The price a facility charges for focus group sessions is the third major problem area for moderators and clients, especially the absolute charge for the sessions, and the hidden costs.

Price Quotes. The prices that facilities quote for a group of sessions, even using the exact same recruiting specifications and facility requirements can vary dramatically, depending on the facility making the bid. The moderator should ensure that the services that the facility is to provide are clearly identified in writing, so that there are no questions about the facility's role. By clearly spelling out the services in writing, the price that a facility quotes will be based on these exact services, resulting with no "surprises."

A moderator can also minimize pricing problems by asking more than one facility to make a bid for the project. This will allow the moderator to compare the costs and any apparent "irregularities" in a bid, then discuss them with the facility that placed the bid. Comparative bidding takes more time, but it is normally the best way to ensure that the costs of facility services are appropriate for the competitive market.

Hidden Costs. The hidden costs for which a facility will charge are typically for things like special food requested on the day of the group, and photocopying, fax machine, and telephone charges. These are legitimate expenses for which a facility should charge its clients, but problems arise when the amount that is charged for the services is too high. For example, some focus group facilities permit their clients to use the copier (within reasonable limits) without cost, whereas others charge between ten and twenty-five cents per page.

The best way to avoid these problems is to ensure that the costs are understood by both the client and the facility in advance. If both parties understand what they will and will not be charged for and how much it costs, there will be no surprises later on.

On balance, pricing can create serious problems in the focus group process if the moderator, client, and facility are not sensitive to one another's needs and feelings. Therefore, the key to successful financial arrangements is openness and discussion, so that both the client and the facility are willing to talk about pricing problems at the time they are raised, before they become damaging to the relationship.

The Ten Commandments: Demands on a Facility

1. Thou shalt recruit participants according to the directions of the client's screening questionnaire, using procedures that eliminate frequent participants and friends from qualifying.
2. Thou shalt deliver full groups of qualified participants for all sessions, regardless of the efforts required to confirm and rescreen the participants who have agreed to come.
3. Thou shalt provide reasonable and competitive pricing for all services, including room rental, recruiting, food, and videotaping.
4. Thou shalt be sensitive to the confidentiality needs of the clients at all times.
5. Thou shalt be sensitive to the need for absolute quiet in the facility while a session is in progress, by soundproofing and by directing employees to be quiet.
6. Thou shalt have focus group and observation rooms that are sufficiently large, comfortable, and well lighted to provide a conducive environment for the research and the observers.
7. Thou shalt control the temperature of the rooms so they are comfortable throughout the sessions.

8. Thou shalt provide hostesses who are professional in their appearance and their interactions with clients and participants.

9 Thou shalt provide effective sound and video systems for the groups, to ensure high-quality recording.

10. Thou shalt pay attention to small but important details like proper preparation of name tags, cleanliness of the rooms, and having easels, sharp pencils, and paper in the rooms during sessions.

Facility Outline

The Services of the Facility
   Participant recruitment
      Recruiting procedures
      Attendence
      Providing directions
   Rescreening participants
   Physical plant
      Reception area
      Focus group room
      Observation room
      Restrooms
   Appropriate support materials
   Audio and/or video support
   Food for participants and clients
   Assurance of confidentiality
   Financial and administrative requirements
   Miscellaneous responsibilities
      Photocopying
      Telephone and fax services
      Sample product pickup
      Product disposal
      Moderator recommendations
      Hotel and restaurant recommendations
Common Problems
   Facility problems
      Room quality
      Noise level
   Recruitment problems
      No-shows
      Unqualified participants
      "Professional" respondents
      Late arrivals
   Pricing problems
      Price quotes
      Hidden costs

Glossary

Anthropomorphic—a moderation technique in which participants describe a product or service in terms of a human being. The objective of this vehicle is to permit the moderator to probe the participants' feelings about the product or service by giving the inanimate object life, personality, and lifestyle.

At-home testing—a procedure in which a participant is provided with a product sample to use at home before a group session, so that he or she will be more knowledgeable about it and be better prepared to discuss it during the session. The procedure can also be used after a session, when a product sample is provided to a participant with the agreement that he or she will be telephoned to follow up on his or her reaction to the item.

Attitudinal scaling—a moderation technique that focuses on the two most important characteristics of a product or service. Participants are instructed to conceptualize the product or service on a two-dimensional scale, such as price and quality, side effects and efficacy, or speed and cost. This helps the moderator delve deeper into the participants' feelings about the product or service.

Audiotaping—the audiotape recording of focus group proceedings. Virtually all group sessions are audiotaped.

Back room—the observation room from which client personnel watch and listen to focus group proceedings through a one-way mirror.

Bid—the estimate a facility provides to a client or moderator, covering the cost of the group session(s). Normally a bid includes the cost of recruiting, co-op payments, room rental, and food. A moderator's charge for conducting focus groups could also be a bid. The term *bid* usually involves getting prices from different suppliers for a particular job.

Briefing—a meeting in which a client provides a moderator with sufficient background information about a research project so that the moderator can recommend the most appropriate research methodology and, if focus groups are called for, begin to prepare for them. A briefing may be either a face-to-face interaction or a telephone conversation.

Co-op—the payment provided to participants as an incentive to come to the focus groups. The amount varies dramatically, based on the difficulty of recruiting the participants.

Conceptual mapping—a moderation technique in which participants are asked to place the names of products or services on a grid. How they group the items on the diagram is used to stimulate discussion.

Conclusions—the section of the final report that contains the moderator's interpretation of the output from the group sessions, in light of the research objectives.

Conjoint association—a moderation technique in which participants are asked to choose between two hypothetical products or services, each of which has different attributes. The objective is to stimulate discussion about the various attributes in order to gain insight into the relative value of each.

Data base—the computerized list of people whom a facility has identified as willing to participate in a session sometime in the future. Normally, a database contains basic demographic data (like age, income, and occupation) and selective product usage information. This enables the facility to recruit qualified persons for focus group sessions relatively easily. The number of people listed varies dramatically, but most facilities in metropolitan areas have in excess more than five thousand names, in order to be able to provide "fresh," qualified respondents.

Demographics—the objective and quantifiable characteristics of consumers by which they are classified into groups. Demographic designators include age, marital status, income, family size, and occupation, among many others.

Discussion guide—*see* Guide.

Duplicate number validation—an emerging service in the focus group industry in which the names and telephone numbers of people recruited for groups are submitted to a central screening organization *in advance* of the groups for the purpose of screening out people who have recently participated in any session or are involved in focus groups more frequently than is desired.

Dyad—a qualitative research methodology in which an interviewer works with two participants at once. This technique is particularly appropriate for products and services for which two persons are relatively equal partners in making a purchase decision.

Expressive drawing—a moderation technique in which participants are asked to express their reaction to a product or service by drawing a picture.

External stimuli—objects that are introduced into a focus group to generate reactions from the participants. Examples include concept boards, product proto-types, and rough and finished advertising.

Facility—the organization in whose physical plant the focus groups are held. The traditional setup is a room with a large conference table (that seats ten people comfortably) and an observation room, connected to each other by a one-way mirror. In addition, a facility normally provides a variety of services such as re-cruiting the participants, providing food, procuring competitive product samples, arranging for the videotaping of the sessions, and the like.

Field service—another term for "facility," except not many field services also do quantitative surveys via telephone.

Final report—the document that the moderator develops at the conclusion of focus group sessions. Its length varies, but, a typical final report includes several sections: a summary of the methodology used in the groups, a review of the key findings, and the conclusions or the moderator's *interpretation* of what the find-ings mean in light of the research objectives. Some final reports also contain a recommendations section, which contains the moderator's suggestions for the next steps that the client should take based on the conclusions of the research.

Findings—the portion of the final report wherein the "facts" from the focus groups are summarized. The "Findings" section is normally organized like the moderator guide and covers each of the topics identified in it. It does not interpret the information but *reports* the findings on which the interpretation will be based.

Fixed personality association—a projective moderation technique in which participants are shown pictures of people, places, or things and asked to interpret them in regard to the topic. Fixed personality associations use the same pictures over an extended period of time rather than varying them so that "norms" are created that may apply to a large number of sessions.

Focus group—a qualitative market research technique in which a group of eight to ten participants of common demographics, attitudes, or purchase patterns are led through a (usually) two-hour discussion of a particular topic by a trained mod-erator.

Focus vision—a network of focus group facilities that offer remote broadcasting and two-way communication between a facility and a client's office. This service enables client organizations to observe groups in various parts of the country with-out having to travel.

"Fresh" participants—participants who have never participated in a session previously, or not for several years.

Full group—a focus group with eight to ten participants. A less-than-full group is normally referred to as a minigroup.

Global focus—focus groups conducted using satellite video technology in which participants are located in different places, normally in different countries. (This technique was pioneered by DMB&B and Clarion Marketing and Communications.)

Grid—a graphic provided to focus group participants in conceptual mapping and attitudinal scaling exercises.

Group dynamics—the impact of participants' inputs on one another in a focus group discussion. An effective moderator can enable group dynamics to promote helpful discussion by various techniques, as well as minimize the potentially negative effects of group dynamics.

Guide—the outline that the moderator uses to lead the discussion in the focus group session. It is also called the moderator guide. It is developed by the moderator on the basis of the briefing and identifies the topics that will be covered in a focus group session, and the approximate emphasis that will be given to each. This is the primary way the moderator communicates with the client organization about the anticipated content of the focus group session.

Homogeneous groups—focus groups in which the participants have extremely similar characteristics.

Honorarium—the co-op payment provided to focus group participants. The term *honorarium* is most frequently used when the participants are professionals, such as physicians, lawyers, and architects.

Hostess—the individual (male or female) responsible for greeting the participants as they arrive at the facility and for preparing the room. The hostess's responsibilities include providing food for the participants and the client observers, rescreening respondents when they arrive, preparing of nametags, and the like.

In-house recruiting—the recruiting of participants by telephone solicitations from people who are physically located within the facility. Most moderators prefer in-house recruiting as it allows them more control over the recruiting process.

Incentive—the co-op payment to participants for coming to a focus group.

Incidence—the percentage of people in a population who qualify for a focus group, based on the specifications that have been developed. The higher the incidence, the less expensive it is to recruit participants for a focus group.

Intercept—a recruitment method in which an interviewer stops (or "intercepts") people in a mall or other public location and administers a brief series of screening questions to them.

Interviewer—the person responsible for recruiting participants for a focus group.

Laddering—a probing technique, used in one-on-ones and focus groups, designed to delve into the "real" reasons for participants' attitudes and behavior toward the topic. It is generally considered to be an intensive technique. The moderator seeks the reason behind each answer until he or she arrives at a basic human need such as ego or status.

Lists—names of customers, former customers, suppliers, or industry influentials that clients sometimes provide to interviewers, from which participants are to be recruited for focus groups.

Mall intercept—*see* Intercept.

Methodology—the section of the final report in which the moderator outlines the approach used in the research, including the method of recruiting participants, the location of the groups, the external stimuli used, and so on. *Methodology* can also mean the approach a moderator uses to conduct the sessions.

Minigroup—a focus group that contains between four to six participants. More than six is normally considered a "full group," and fewer than four is a triad or a dyad.

Mixed groups—a focus group that contains both males and females. Most moderators prefer to work with groups that are not mixed.

Moderator guide—*see* Guide.

No-show—a focus group participant who agrees to come to a session and is confirmed the same day, but nonetheless does not come to the group. Facilities compensate for no-shows by overrecruiting for groups by two or three people.

Notes—the summary information that observers develop during focus groups. Normally, notes are only their most important comments written in a shorthand format.

Observation room—*see* Back room.

One-on-one—a qualitative research technique in which a moderator interviews one participant, normally behind a one-way mirror.

One-way mirror—a special mirror that permits observers to watch the proceedings in the group without the participants being able to see the observers. Virtually all focus groups are conducted in a room separated from an observation area by a one-way mirror.

Overrecruit—the extra people who are recruited for a focus group to compensate for the inevitable "no-shows."

Participant—a person included in a focus group.

People board—a moderation technique in the class of fixed personality associations, developed by Tom Greenbaum of Clarion Marketing and Communications. Participants are exposed to a permanent display of photographs of people of various ages, socioeconomic levels, and ethnic groups, which enables the moderator to delve further into the thoughts and feelings of the participants about the topic being discussed. The advantage of this fixed personality association over variable personality associations is that norms of participants' reactions to each image are established over time, which helps the moderator interpret participants' reactions and indicates areas to probe during the discussions.

"Professional" respondent—a participant who attends many sessions by volunteering for the recruitment lists of different facilities. Most moderators seek to eliminate "professional" respondents from groups, since they do not generally respond in the same objective way that "fresh" respondents do but tend to try to anticipate what they think moderators want to hear.

Projectability—the capability of research results to be extrapolated to the larger universe, on the assumption that the sample is representative of the total. Focus groups are sometimes criticized because, as a qualitative methodology, their results are not projectable due to the small sample sizes involved and the selectiveness of participant recruitment.

Projective—a class of moderation techniques used to stimulate discussion among participants. These techniques force the participants to think about the topic in a more subjective or creative way than they might in a "normal" discussion. Projectives discussed in this book include sentence completion, expressive drawing, anthropomorphization and associations.

Qualitative research—research whose objective is to gain insight into attitudes and feelings, not to develop numerical data that may be projectable to a larger universe. Qualitative methodologies include focus groups, minigroups, and one-on-ones.

Quantitative research—research designed to generate projectable numerical data about a topic. Quantitative studies are conducted by telephone, mail, or interviews.

Quota—a minimum number of focus group participants who must meet certain criteria. A moderator might set a quota of having half group be users of Brand X, or one-third be aware of Product Y.

Random selection—a selection process in which everyone has an equal chance of being chosen for participation. Random recruiting is the ideal for respondents for both qualitative and quantitative studies. But due to cost considerations, only a small percentage of all quantitative research conducted uses purely random sampling. For focus group sessions, recruitment is almost never random.

Recommendations—the section of the final report that suggests the next action steps a client could take, based on the conclusions of the research.

Recruiter—*see* Interviewer.

Recruitment—the process of securing participants for focus groups.

Release forms—the form that some clients and facilities ask participants to sign to release them from all responsibility for any consequences of the groups. These are most often signed when participants will taste food or beverages, particularly alcohol, or tobacco products.

Rescreening—a brief interview conducted with potential participants when they arrive at a facility to ensure that they really qualify for the session. Rescreening normally uses some of the questions that were originally asked when the participants were originally recruited.

Respondent—*see* Participant.

Sample—the participants in a focus group, as research subjects.

Screener—the screening questionnaire used to recruit participants. Most moderators review the screener before a session to become familiar with the participant types and to ensure that the recruitment has been correct.

Screening—*see* Recruitment.

Sentence completion—a moderation technique in which participants are asked to finish a sentence that has been started for them. The purpose of this technique is to enable participants to delve into certain areas that they may otherwise find difficult to discuss.

Sign-out sheets—a control document used by a facility to keep track of co-op payments to participants.

Specifications—the criteria for participants in a focus group, involving their demographic characteristics, product usage, product awareness, and so on.

Syndicated research—research conducted on behalf of more than one client, who share the costs.

Target consumers—the type of people who are to participate in a focus group. *See* Specifications.

Telephone groups—a qualitative research methodology in which seven to ten people are connected in a telephone conference call and a trained moderator leads them through a discussion about a particular topic. Telephone groups are typically used with people who normally would not communicate with each other due to competitive conflicts but who will participate in an anonymous telephone discussion.

Triad—a qualitative research methodology in which a moderator works with three respondents. Some researchers maintain that the limited number of participants in a triad permits the moderator to get more information from them than is possible in a minigroup of full group.

Value-added—the extra value a moderator brings to a client by virtue of his or her previous training or experience.

Variable personality association—a moderation technique in which photographs are selected for a particular focus group, to secure participants' reactions to a particular topic that they represent. The "variable" aspect of this technique is that the photos are tailored to the group rather than *fixed,* as in the People Board.

Verbatim—a transcript of the actual comments participants make in a focus group. Many moderators include verbatims in their final reports, to support their interpretation of the finding.

Video focus groups—*see* Global Focus.

Viewing room—*see* Back Room.

Write-down—the process of having participants write down their views on a topic during a focus group. Moderators use write-downs to get participants to commit to their point of view before other participants can influence them.

Index